LESSONS
on the Road to
Financial
Independence

H. Michael Finkle

iUniverse, Inc.
Bloomington

Lessons on the Road to Financial Independence

iUniverse books may be ordered through booksellers or by contacting:

iUniverse
1663 Liberty Drive
Bloomington, IN 47403
www.iuniverse.com
1-800-Authors (1-800-288-4677)

ISBN: 978-1-4620-8356-5 (sc)
ISBN: 978-1-4620-8357-2 (hc)
ISBN: 978-1-4620-8358-9 (e)

Library of Congress Control Number: 2011962923

Printed in the United States of America

iUniverse rev. date: 5/7/2012

This work is dedicated to Judi, Jennifer, and Scott
—the best spouse and children one could ever hope for.

Contents

Preface

I have worked as an investment advisor for forty-four years, having worked for six different investment firms, three of which were merged into other larger investment houses during my tenure. It has been my good fortune to have consistently been in the top asset-and-revenue tier of my company for the past thirty-some years even though, on three separate occasions, I have brought in business partners with whom I have shared some of my client relationships or split my book of business.

My approach to clients has often been described as that of a teacher, and I spent the better part of twenty years intermittently teaching "Principals of Investing" as an adult education course in a local community college. I found this endeavor very rewarding. Frankly, I enjoy the interaction with other professionals who use this manner of relating to me, for at heart I believe that I am a lifelong student who likes to understand not only what I am doing but why I am doing it.

Over the course of my career, I have been fortunate to be cited by three national trade publications as one of the nation's top financial advisors.* Being recognized by one's peers of course always feels good, but more

---

*   *Research* magazine named H. Michael Finkle as one of six inductees
     into their "Broker Hall of Fame" in 1992. *Registered Rep* named him
     to receive their "Outstanding Broker Award" in May 1993. He was
     also cited by*Medical Economics* as one of the "150 Best Financial
     Advisors for Doctors" in 2008, 2009, and 2010.

importantly, it makes me even more acutely aware of my obligations to both my clients and the business I work in.

I have tried to not write a narrow, technically detailed, how-to-invest book. Instead I have attempted to address the goal of seeking personal financial independence first by sharing my personal background story, followed by relating my investment experiences, values, and advice, in the belief that many individual investors can relate to it and gain from one individual's long-term perspective, using my views and experience as a springboard to formulate their own road map to use in seeking personal financial independence. Of course, some parts of this work do naturally address more specific investment ideas for illustration purposes.

My goal is to deliver a message of practical hope for those who are truly dedicated and realistic in the pursuit of financial independence and to inspire you to rededicate yourself to your life's goals and personal values. This is a story and message of personal discipline tempered by the world's often harsh realities and seasoned by the realization that life is a journey, not a destination or simply a money-centered undertaking. Believe it or not, there can be a spiritual side to your financial quest and it can make all the difference in your life and the lives of those around you. One of my great joys has been to see disciplined middle-class savers become financially independent investors through persistent dedication to their goals, in the finest American tradition of thrift, hard work, and risk taking. They finance America!

Introduction

Financial independence *is a term generally used to describe the state of having sufficient personal wealth to live indefinitely without having to work actively for basic necessities.**

Having been both an individual investor and an investment advisor for nearly five decades, I have always related to the goal of achieving personal financial independence. In fact, this was my own goal as far back as my early twenties, but it grew even more over time as my life experiences reinforced the desirability, even the necessity, of pursuing financial independence.

I believe that pursuing financial independence is one of the few ways you can attempt to control your own destiny because it provides freedom from so many of the world's forces over which you have absolutely no control. Don't misunderstand my intent. I have nothing against work; in fact I love work. I think life is all about meaningful work which, at the end of the day or at the end of your life for that matter, allows you to reflect and say, "Today I provided my best efforts to achieve a fair return, and as a result, I received a balanced and fair outcome."

Born to parents who came of age in the heart of the Great Depression and who faced very difficult life circumstances, I never doubted—even as a youngster—that I would work all of my life. I was always

---

*   www.wikipedia.org (September 14, 2009).

encouraged to give my best efforts to succeed at whatever level I could attain. More than once my mother would say, "I don't care if you are a ditchdigger; just be the best ditchdigger that you can be." Of course I knew that she wanted me to achieve more, but I got the message and obediently followed those instructions throughout my life. I also suspect that having a strong competitive nature contributed to my falling in line with this parental guidance.

My early life formed the foundation of my lifelong interest in financial matters. I believe that correctly pursuing financial independence can lead to a life more fully lived and can open doors to an even more rewarding life experience. Please note that I said a "more rewarding life experience" and not a "more rewarding destination," for I firmly believe that life is a journey not a destination. This life is not a dress rehearsal. There are no mulligans or do-overs. What we do every day with the time allotted to us is our call. This is our one and only earthly life, and if you find yourself, as I did, in circumstances where a life of work to support yourself economically is inevitable, then accept that fact and get on with it. You and I did not and will not inherit wealth which will support us. Instead we have been given opportunity.

Steeped in this tradition, I was primed to accept what I learned in college as Hegel's dialectic materialism and the belief that one's destiny is worked out in the material world. The Protestant work ethic seemed very real to me and validated my young worldview. It also seemed to me that Hegel's concept of thesis versus antithesis leading to synthesis was perfectly logical and explained how the world worked and how Western mankind evolved.

When I became an investment advisor and needed to find clients, I convinced the local community college to allow me to teach an adult education course about investing. Teaching enabled me—actually forced me—to organize my thoughts and truly build the case for pursuing financial independence as well as the strategies that I believed would help anyone have a real shot at reaching this goal. Most of the concepts I used in those classes, which eventually ran for nearly twenty years, were compiled in a small book I published back in 1974 entitled, *Investing: The Permanent Problem of Protecting Capital* (Adams Press). Now, many years later, most of those financial concepts still work, and some of the word pictures I tried to paint can still help anyone in pursuit of our shared goal.

Although I have considered writing this book for several years now, my wife finally convinced me to carry out this endeavor with several goals in mind. The first goal is to share with the reader my belief that influences and forces we encounter early in our formative years will shape us just as my early life experiences shaped my determination to succeed. Hopefully this simple example can be used by readers to reinforce their own efforts to propel their lives on a positive trajectory. A second and critical goal is to urge readers to accumulate all of their life experiences into a set of core values and beliefs that will ultimately prepare them to exploit the inevitable inflection points that life and history can present to them as a major opportunity.

Just as the inflation-racked exorbitant interest rate period of 1980–1982 presented me with an opportunity of a lifetime, today's global financial malaise may be providing another once-in-a-lifetime opportunity for a reader who grasps the potential within this dour scene and can exploit it to their own (and society's) betterment. This mind-set is based on the belief that all coins have two sides and opposite every problem or challenge is an opportunity for someone to benefit from.

Finally on a purely personal note, I hope that this work might provide inspiration for youngsters like my grandchildren, so that they can be exposed to a formal guide to one family's heritage and insight into how that one family both built and lived their values and their lives. Youngsters need to know that they can rise to whatever level they can aspire to if they will pay the personal price for getting there. I know it sounds trite to some, but I believe that America was built by individuals who did not accept conventional wisdom or succumb to the belief that they could not improve their lot in life. They defined financial independence in their own terms often without ever uttering those exact words, but they knew it when they experienced or imagined it.

As you read the pages that follow, please understand that I am focused on and write about the attainment of material success. But don't lose sight of the fact that I believe that achieving this goal will not in and of itself lead to a successful or personally fulfilling life. That will occur only if along the way in this lifetime journey, you take the opportunities which will inevitably appear as either teachable or learnable moments and use them for nonmaterial rewards and achievements.

May you and yours truly experience a life worth living and emulating.

CHAPTER 1

Financial Independence: Beginnings

I was fortunate to be born into a hardworking, ambitious family right at the beginning of World War II. My parents had their individual challenges and burdens to bear, but they were smart and self-sufficient.

As a child, my father lived in an apartment above the general store that his parents owned and operated. He grew up in a small town in Iowa, to which his family had migrated from Chicago. However, I always viewed his existence as similar to that of a kid living in a large, urban ethnic neighborhood where everyone on the block knew everyone else, and all struggled to scrape out an existence. Behind his house was an alley that separated his yard from a junkyard. My father sometimes regaled my brother and me with stories of selling junk metal to the junkyard owner, often for pennies. Over the years, he used the money he accumulated from this and other entrepreneurial activities to buy fireworks to sell at his annual Fourth of July fireworks stand. Apparently this entrepreneur ran a very profitable stand, for he eventually accumulated enough money to build a new home for himself and his bride in 1940, spending the enormous sum of $4,000 on the endeavor. His own father thought he was absolutely crazy to put his life savings into a home and told him so, but my father was determined to provide a life for his family away from the downtown flat he knew growing up.

At a very early age, I learned directly from my father the virtues of hard work and thrift. He was an interesting blend of prudent businessman and speculator. He was basically very conservative when it came to personal finances, but at the same time willing to take what for him were very large gambles on new ventures. As an ambitious kid who could sell anything, he, like others of his generation, escaped the Depression era through a combination of intelligence, diligence, ambition, and the willingness to risk greatly, but only after careful consideration of all the potential outcomes. He also had great intuition when it came to reading other people.

My mother, on the other hand, had a much tougher childhood. Her father was a brick mason who ran his own masonry company but had a weakness for spirits, and that nearly ruined their lives. A hardworking German immigrant, he knew the life of hard labor and just rewards. However, his drinking drove him to abandon his family, and my mother, who was only thirteen or fourteen at the time, became the "mother" of her family, overseeing her three siblings while her own mother went to work as a seamstress to support them. Forced to move in with their widowed grandfather, my mother bore the psychological scars of her father's rejection all of her life and was willing to make any sacrifice to see that her own children never faced life without the support and encouragement of two functioning parents in the home.

I share this story of my parents' lives for one reason. It seemed to me that my parents lived the creed that being poor or struggling was an advantage, not a handicap. I was never sure that they really believed that, but in many ways they communicated that belief to me as I was growing up and even after reaching adulthood. I have always believed that knowing where you come from and who you are can be a source of inner strength and ambition. And the world I heard about and knew as a boy was not exactly rosy.

When you listen to your forebears talk about the world of the 1930s Depression and eking out a hand-to-mouth living, you vicariously live parts of their lives and come to realize that you are truly on your own economically. That stark reality shaped my life on several levels. I did not lose my small savings in the bank failures of 1932 like my paternal grandfather, but I might as well have after listening to several soft-spoken conversations between my father and his father.

The central point here is that I was overtly and covertly taught that you and I are adrift in the economic seas. Through the focused application of all of our various personal resources, we have the opportunity and yes, the need, to chart our own course seeking financial independence at whatever level we can reach, in this onetime-only crapshoot called life. That does not mean money is our only life goal—far from it. Material wealth will not necessarily make us happy, but neither will poverty. If we view money as a tool to help us achieve something better, both materially and spiritually, then we may have found one key to successfully navigating life.

Remember that money is a tool and only a tool. How we use it is the question at hand. In the following pages, we will together explore my perspective on how to manage this tool successfully.

Before we leave this discussion, I want to share one final thought about the benefits of adversity. As young college students, my fraternity brothers and I often attended services at the First Methodist Church, as the minister was one of the best public speakers I had ever heard. To this day, I rank Frank Nessler as among the best. The following statement from one of his Sunday sermons was seared into my brain forever: "Remember, the same flame that melts butter, hardens steel." Needless to say, I got it and believe it with all my heart, then and today.

LESSONS FOR YOUR ROAD TO FINANCIAL INDEPENDENCE:

✓ Adversities—real, imagined, or inherited—can be an inspiration and a source of strength.

✓ The search for financial independence requires real work and determination.

CHAPTER 2

Money as a Tool

We begin our discussion of money as a tool by asking you to drop the belief that simply making more money can lead you to financial independence. It won't. If it were that simple, every high-salaried professional athlete in the world would finish his career financially independent. Trust me, too often that is not the case. In fact, many of yesterday's multimillion-dollar athletes are financially destitute. It is frequently the same story for lottery winners or those who receive large legal settlements. They are likely to end up broke or nearly so.

Why is it that earning more money does not result in achieving financial independence? In my experience, the answer begins with lack of discipline and not having a plan or system.

Think of your income as a pie. It is yours to slice anyway you wish, but simply earning more or having a larger pie will not get you there. Of course, the size of your income pie matters, but it is only the first consideration.

It is my contention that there are only three things you can do with your income pie: you can spend, you can save or invest, or you can pay taxes. We cannot alter the size of any of these slices without proportionately changing the size of another. So, if we choose to spend more, we would have less to save and invest, and conversely, if we elect to invest more, we must reduce spending or taxes or both.

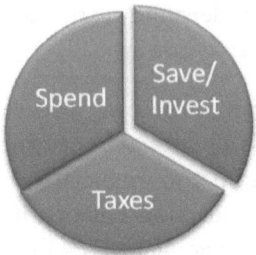

To achieve financial independence, we must not only seek a larger income pie, but we also have to exercise as much control as possible over the three major slices.

This simple concept is an important key to your journey toward financial independence. It is really that simple, and it is really that stark. I would argue that living in the greatest consumptive society the world has ever known can be both a blessing and a curse. Just trust me when I say that in America today, you can spend whatever you make regardless of the amount. We have taken personal consumption to a new level, having long ago far surpassed what had previously been considered an adequate standard of living. A cynical economist might express this by claiming that consumption always rises to match the amount of money available to be consumed.

Of course, the desire to improve our living standards has driven mankind for centuries. The yearning to escape the grinding poverty of rural China or India today is not unlike the driving force that early generations of Americans endured on the road to a better material life, and so be it. While that natural drive for more and better is basic to all mankind, our focus here is on the goal of accumulating sufficient financial resources to support ourselves when we are no longer able to earn a living, or earlier in life if we can create that outcome.

Because of the world we live in, this pursuit is not only noble but necessary. Over the years, it has been my privilege to speak to various service, educational, or financial audiences. Beginning in the early 1980s, almost every one of those presentations has begun with the following statement: "You and I are in competition every day with everyone else in the world, for everything. If you do not believe that, I do not know what planet you are living on." Today, most Americans would have no problem understanding this statement immediately, but that was not the case thirty years ago.

If you have adopted this worldview, you understand why seeking financial independence is a personal imperative. For the most part, the days of finding meaningful and financially rewarding work for those who have little formal education have ended in advanced Western countries. The experience of going to work for a company and staying in that company until retirement is now the exception, not the rule. And very few members of today's workforce expect to receive a defined benefit pension. Rather, our typical retirement plan is a defined contribution plan, and we accumulate what we contribute financially, not what a benevolent employer bestows upon us at the end of our careers.

I discovered years ago that some people are totally turned off by what I call "the saving thing." You know the lingo as well as I do: "You only live once." "There are no guarantees in life." "I want to live while I can still enjoy life." Each of these statements has some ring of truth, but I come back to the reality that financially, you and I are on our own—period. If the terms *saving* or *investing* do not resonate with you, could I soften it by suggesting that you use the phrase "deferred consumption" instead? That's right. Saving and investing can be described simply as deferring consumption of that particular piece of your financial pie until later.

I must insert here that my life's work—advising others how to plan for their future and invest their money—has led me to conclude that there are really only two types of people in the world—spenders and savers. I have also noticed that savers often marry spenders, but that is a discussion for another day. An economist might say that individuals have either a propensity to save or a propensity to spend. The point here is that we need to understand and manage whatever our personal inclination might be. I confess to being a disproportionate saver and always have been, with no memory of ever spending all that I earned in any given year—ever. That I am not alone has been well documented by academics like Dr. Thomas Stanley, author of *The Millionaire Next Door*, and others who document that saving leads to success.

Let's recap. To achieve financial independence, we need to earn more over time; to save and invest as much as we can, balancing today's needs with tomorrow's financial realities; and to pay as little in taxes as legally possible.

At a minimum, I strongly urge anyone with the opportunity to participate in an employer-sponsored retirement plan, such as a 401(k) plan, to contribute as much as possible. You will defer taxes on money that otherwise would be currently taxed and can invest what would have been tax money until you begin withdrawals later in life. This is a great example of changing the size of the slices in your income pie as you save more by paying less in current taxes.

Controlling current taxes can also be accomplished by using federally tax-exempt municipal bonds and tax-deferred annuities for those who are aggressively saving and investing after-tax money. Municipal bonds can eliminate current taxes on income while annuities defer taxes. I have used both approaches with great success over many years—for my own investing and for many clients.

In summary, money is your tool for achieving your goal. If you want financial self-sufficiency, aggressively saving and investing over time is critical to reaching your destination. Remember that financial independence can be achieved on many different levels and individuals can determine their own level. For further insights on this, I strongly recommend that you get a copy of the book, *The Number*, by Lee Eisenberg. This is a great read by a very accomplished writer who shares with the reader his own search for the magic number that most would define simply as, "How much money do I need to support myself?" We are not talking about *rich* here as that word is so relative as to be meaningless in this discussion. What we are talking about is defining the standard of living you are targeting, followed by a quantitative analysis of how much capital it might take to support that standard and then applying a range of potential outcomes and time frames to the number. This explanation is oversimplified, but you get the word picture I'm sure and have formed at least a broad general sense of the analytic process that should underlie your financial plan. It will help immensely to earn a great deal of money, but we reiterate that is not the key to your goal. What you do with that income is just as important or even more important.

Finally, let the time value of money work for you. The more you save early in the game, the better your chances for success. I will go so far as to say that how much you save and how early you do so is more important than the rate of return you earn on that money. I am in the investment business and have successfully invested my own and my clients' money for decades, but I am acutely aware that I cannot find an investment with a high enough rate of return to make up for the lack of commitment to "the saving thing" early in life. Just as a cardiologist has no pill to quickly offset years of poor diet and lack of exercise, you will have no more than what you are able to save and invest over a lifetime. While good genes can play a role in physical health, I don't think they make a difference in our financial health.

LESSONS FOR YOUR ROAD TO FINANCIAL INDEPENDENCE:

✓ A substantial income does not automatically result in a high net worth.

✓ Financial self-control and personal dedication to saving and investing are keys to success.

✓ Learning to save and invest early in life is critical to long-term success for most of us.

CHAPTER 3

You Are the Product and Your Most Valuable Asset

If you, like the vast majority of us, are destined to live a lifetime of working either for yourself or someone else, how do you view yourself in that role?

Today organizations of all types are focused on finding employees who can work effectively in teams, and many will hire only those they perceive to be team players. Business teams can be beneficial not just for the organization or employer but also for the employees themselves.

Having first decided to adopt this structure for my own business many years ago, I can testify to the effectiveness of well-constructed business teams. My experience has also taught me that team-building is one of the most difficult challenges facing businesses today. There are numerous examples of success in this endeavor among Japanese companies, and it may be that Japan is a more fertile cultural environment for this approach to business. But there are also many domestic examples of organizations which operate very effectively using teams. As I have seen in my own business, a key component to successful team-building is bringing together people with complementary, not duplicative skills.

However valuable teams may be, I want to encourage you to think about your own personal and financial goals and how best to achieve them. How important is it for you to have options in your life and achieve some degree of financial independence? We are not talking about lip service to these goals but a real commitment to achieving them. If you embrace financial independence as your primary goal, I believe you also have to commit to independent thinking and acting. This does not mean that you cannot be an effective member of a successful business unit or team, but it does mean that in the end, if forced to make a choice, you will probably select serving your own goals rather than the team's goals.

Does that make you unfit to work in a collaborative environment? Absolutely not. Nobel economist Milton Friedman has said that society is advanced by each individual pursuing his own enlightened self-interest. Of course, some may argue that this is a selfish approach, but the counterargument is that individuals pursuing their enlightened self-interest better serve themselves and society generally.

If you buy into this line of thinking and are committed to pursuing the general goal this book addresses, you may want to adopt the attitude of a free-agent athlete. As a member of your team, you must devote your efforts to the team's winning (or achieving), but you should not make your personal goals subordinate to those of the team. Rather, strive to be the very best or most effective member of that team, while expecting the others to adopt the same attitude of excellence and exceptionalism. Would you prefer to be a member of a team of mediocre players or one of a group of extraordinarily successful people who pursue the twin goals of outstanding achievement individually, as well as a member of the larger group? The answer is obvious, isn't it?

I would go so far as to say that there can probably be a basic conflict between you and your goal of achieving personal financial independence and the goal of many work arenas where you will be forced to work in a team setting where the success of the team is paramount. If you can manage that potential conflict, I suspect that you will be successful on both the team and individual fronts, but it is hard to subdue the extraordinary inner drive that a committed individual goal seeker develops. To attack this potential conflict between individual and group goals, consider adopting the attitude that you are the work product.

Why does it matter that you view yourself as a "product"? It matters because, all other things being equal, in the end you as the product are for sale to the highest bidder. You sell your skills and services (your product) in pursuit of your personal fulfillment and goals. And, you can decide for yourself that you will not work for unethical, incompetent, or even mediocre people or organizations. Instead, you can choose to work only for the brightest and the best and reserve the right to walk out the door the moment that organization is no longer as just described or will no longer reward you sufficiently.

Refer back for a moment to the reference made earlier to the free-agent athlete mentality. Isn't the attitude just described above compatible with that of a free-agent athlete who is willing to give his all for the team because winning is measured by the team not by individuals? At the same time, it is equally true that our hypothetical athlete is for sale to the highest bidder. He knows that he will only have peak performance and earning skills for a relatively short period of time, so he must maximize the pursuit of his goals in that time period.

Most of us have a work life longer then that of most professional athletes, but is your situation really that much different if you are one of those individuals who has the financial independence goal stenciled on your forehead so to speak?

If you think that this attitude is too harsh or unrealistic or selfish, ask yourself these questions: Do you believe that most businesses in today's world really care about you as a person? Would they hesitate to throw you under the bus in pursuit of their corporate goals?

If you cannot find an organization that meets your high standards, build one yourself if you have the entrepreneurial drive and stamina to do so. Use your own enlightened self-interest to improve yourself and society.

LESSONS FOR YOUR ROAD TO FINANCIAL INDEPENDENCE:

✓ You can pursue your personal financial goals while working collaboratively.

✓ You can and should expect your collaborators to measure up to your standards of excellence.

CHAPTER 4

Does Seeking Financial Independence Mean Seeking to Retire?

Financial independence isn't necessarily the same as retirement, although it can be. I believe seeking financial independence means seeking choices in one's life. It is that simple. One choice could be to retire from what we normally call work, but it does not necessarily mean leaving work to sit on the couch. If that is your goal, so be it, but it could be a shortcut to the mortuary.

No doubt many become physically or mentally worn out, and health issues may force us to move to a life no longer dominated by getting out of bed each day and heading off to a remote work site or for that matter to the home office. What we are talking about is creating choices.

We have already expressed the view that life is about work—but meaningful and rewarding work. Work provides structure, and most human beings need structure in their lives. In fact, daily structure may be all that keeps many of us effectively functioning.

On the other hand, after decades of working, some of us long for a much more freely structured or even a basically unstructured life.

Part of my life's work has involved advising people as they plan for their own retirement time. My standard recommendation to everyone thinking about the "R" word is to go *to* something, not *from* something. No matter what that destination may be, you should have a plan or an ideal activity or a desire to do something that is meaningful to you.

It is also smart to test-drive those destination activities. If you think that you want to paint, try it now. Take a class. Join the local art league. Attend art lectures. Enroll in a community college or college art appreciation or painting class. Make friends with someone who is already practicing what you think you might want to do. You may find that painting is truly fulfilling and interesting, or you may decide it is an imaginary oasis and not what you thought it would be. It is far better to learn that now rather than after you have chucked it all for an easel and brushes, only to find that is not what you really want.

We would be remiss not to point out another life option that might fall under the heading of financial independence being achieved in midlife by someone who has made sufficient money but has no interest in retiring. For instance, there are examples out there of gifted surgeons who gave up the big group practice to go practice in remote areas of underdeveloped countries or in the nation's inner-city neighborhoods. They use their financial resources to underwrite what may be economic underemployment to pursue more personal or socially fulfilling lives, thus living their individual versions of financial independence.

I also know "retired" individuals who expend more energy on Habitat for Humanity home building then they did in their previous work lives and are very happy doing so. These volunteer carpenters are sometimes fulfilling a lifetime dream of physically building something tangible.

LESSONS FOR YOUR ROAD TO FINANCIAL INDEPENDENCE:

- ✓ Financial independence means being able to make choices for your life.
- ✓ Retirement could be one of those personal choices, but investigate and plan well beforehand to have an active and meaningful "Act III."

CHAPTER 5

Exploiting Long-Wave Opportunities

For the first five years after I finished college, I worked in various sales and marketing positions with a major public utility company, beginning in their corporate headquarters and later transferring to two different branch regions called service areas. Overall, it was a good experience. I established a reputation as a very effective salesperson, but after four years, I realized that my future there was limited.

Throughout that period of my life, I retained a strong interest in investing, which had begun in college. My best social friend, apart from my work associates, was a young stockbroker in the St. Louis area where we lived at that time. One day as that friend and I were discussing future opportunities, he said, "Has it ever dawned on you that you talk about investing all the time? That is your real interest, so why don't you go into the investment business?"

Ironically, my own father, a lifelong investor in the stock market, had resigned his position as a large department store manager for Carson Pirie Scott of Chicago just a few years earlier, and opened a branch brokerage office for a small Midwest Stock Exchange member firm. He had moved to the top of his retail firm, rising from a furniture department salesman and manager to managing the second largest store in the Carson chain outside of Chicago. But he had become extremely discouraged as he fought company policies that ultimately drove what had been their most profitable operation into the red. Finally, he could no longer stand it and decided to turn his long-term hobby into his business.

By the time I entered the investment business five years later, in August 1967, the stock market was at or near the end of a multiyear bull market, making my timing not the most advantageous. I had spent the previous couple of years attending brokerage firm investment seminars in the St. Louis metro area and listening to brokers from Merrill Lynch and A. G. Edwards pitch their wares to the general public.

My decision to go into the investment business, much encouraged by my broker friend, was also greatly influenced by my father's midlife career change. I greatly admired my father, but he was a demanding and hard-nosed man who usually saw the negative rather than the positive side of things. I had never in my wildest dreams considered working with him. In fact, while in college, on my way to becoming the first college graduate in my immediate family, I had decided that he could accept me and approve of my life or not, and that I really did not care which he did. Much later, I realized that adopting that mind-set probably was what made it possible for me to work with him. Even though at times we saw the world very differently, we always respected the other's point of view.

When I went to ask his advice about my consideration of a career in the investment field and told him that I had spoken with a Merrill Lynch representative (at that time the firm was Merrill, Lynch, Pierce, Fenner & Smith), about joining them, he was encouraging. However, he did point out to me that I would have a very tough go of it trying to build a clientele in the area where I had been living for four years, as my contacts in that community were limited. I was also acutely aware that as a young-looking man in my late twenties, I would have to gain credibility with people much older than I, as my contemporaries had little in the way of investable assets. However, while I was both serious and determined, the initial challenges were indeed daunting for a twenty-seven-year-old with a stay-at-home wife and two young children to feed.

Finally, after months of thinking and discussion, my wife and I decided to take the plunge, and I agreed to begin a self-study program to become a broker with Tabor Securities based in Decatur, Illinois. I remained in my job at the utility company for several months while I studied on weekends and evenings for the qualifying exam to legally sell securities, and I read everything I could lay my hands on about my newly chosen field.

Once the exam was passed, I resigned from my job, put my house on the market, and moved to Danville, Illinois, where I had lived from the age of ten through college. I joined my father, whose business had grown to the point where it appeared survival was less of an issue, and help was needed for it to continue to grow.

On several levels, I never would have dreamed of making this choice, but it worked for all of us. Some years later, as my father and I drifted in different directions with our business philosophies, I had to look back at this jump off the high dive and marvel that it had worked at all. Mr. Tabor, who had made his fortune in the grain trade but always wanted to be an investment banker, agreed to pay me $1,000 a month until my commissions repaid him, at which point I would be on my own. For all of the forty-four years that followed, I have never had a salary or guaranteed income. At the time, his offer matched my previous pay at the utility company. While it was the prevailing income level for someone of my age and experience, today it sounds like next to nothing for a family of four. It took me approximately eighteen months to earn what I had been guaranteed as a starting draw, and after that, I was on my own.

The days that followed were challenging to say the least. After spending time on the firm's OTC (over-the-counter) trading desk in Decatur, I began to make as many contacts as I could in Danville and the surrounding area. At that time, Danville was at its zenith as a small-to-midsized industrial city in America's heartland, with companies like General Motors, General Electric, Hyster lift trucks, Bohn Aluminum, and Tee Pak flexing their industrial muscles. The town was thriving. Corporate families were coming and going, driving real-estate values higher and helping to create a vibrant business and social environment. We lived hand to mouth with almost no financial resources, but we had no debt other than our home mortgage and high hopes for the future.

The world changed a great deal in those early years of my career as the Vietnam War heated up and divided the country, creating severe financial strains. Eventually we entered a very dark period which taught me lessons I would carry to today.

While looking for new prospective clients, I soon realized that most of the money in my small-town world was not in the stock market; it was in the local banks. People like my parents, who had grown up in the Depression and had now reached a much higher economic level, were savers, not investors.

As I met and talked with prospective clients, I realized that in my marketplace I could succeed only by getting people to move money out of the banks. In the beginning, I learned that this was easier to achieve by simply offering a better interest rate. We could talk about the stock market or other options later. For that reason and with that background, the years of the early 1970s, although dark by Wall Street standards, were years of opportunity and modest success for me. The sales manager of Tabor understood and loved the bond market. He was an Ivy League grad and a bit of a snob, but he was willing, if not eager, to share some of what he knew about the bond market with an eager young pup who needed marketable ideas. My father and most other brokers at the time couldn't have cared less about the bond market. The action and opportunities were in stocks. I did not necessarily disagree, but I was frankly more cautious, and besides, my prospect universe was not populated by stock market veterans.

And so, it was "harvest season" for me when the so-called Arab oil embargo and other events helped create inflation, the big interest rate run-up, and the subsequent stock market decline of 1973 and 1974. I could offer five-year, AA- or AAA-rated corporate bonds from companies like R. J. Reynolds or American Tobacco with rates in the area of 8.25%, and attract savers who had never done anything but deposit money into a bank before.

I was just successful enough to keep the bills paid and the business assets growing while the stock market endured one of the three great bear markets of my career. That stock market plunge more or less cut the Dow Jones Industrial Average in half over two years, scaring the dickens out of most of the public. But it was accompanied by interest rate opportunities for savers and eventually created great stock bargains for all to pick over. Ultimately, the deep, midseventies' recession paved the way for a huge stock market rally, as interest rates peaked and the recession began to recede.

That first decade or so of my career taught me some important lessons.

First, I learned that stocks could go for a very long period without the broad averages going anywhere, as the period from my official baptism in 1967 to the mid-1970s was like watching paint dry as the Dow went nowhere.

I also learned in the bear market that followed that stocks could go down in value a lot more than most of us thought possible or at least likely.

Finally, I observed firsthand that dramatically changing interest rates had the power to change minds and move capital from one market to another. These lessons eventually led to some major future successes for me and for our clients.

But first, let's look back to the two previous decades beginning in the 1950s when two very interesting gentlemen served terms as chairmen of the Federal Reserve Board and thus became the public face and voice of US monetary policy. They were William McChesney Martin (who served for nineteen years from Truman to Nixon) and later the professorial, pipe-smoking Arthur Burns (chairman from Nixon into the Carter administration). They presided over US monetary policy during a time when it seemed to me they could talk tough about limiting or controlling inflation, but either their words did not match their deeds, or they simply did not mean them or have the tools to deliver on them.

So, rightly or wrongly, I had developed a pretty cynical view of publicly stated Federal Reserve policies and pronouncements about inflation by the time the so-called Jimmy Carter malaise settled over the financial markets beginning in 1978.

Carter had appointed the very tall, cigar-smoking Paul Volcker to replace Burns as the Fed chief in 1979 as US inflationary pressures were surging.

Nevertheless, when Volcker, with his large physical presence, announced in so many words that his mission was to break the back of inflation and inflationary expectations, for whatever reason, I believed him. There was no doubt that we had an inflation problem, for the Consumer Price Index had moved from an already elevated level of 5.75% in 1976 to a totally unsustainable 13.58% for 1980.[*] Meanwhile, interest rates on one-year treasury notes moved from 5.29% in November of 1976 to an unprecedented 14.15% in November 1980.[†]

I believed that Paul Volcker was going to either break the banking system with high interest rates or break inflationary expectations. It turned out to be a watershed moment in my financial career and for me personally.

I had listened ad nauseam to others talk about how their leveraged investments in commercial real estate were paying off big time as inflation drove prices higher. I had been approached in 1979 by a leading realtor in our community who wanted to sell me an apartment building that he assured me would go up in value because of inflation. I patiently listened to his well-polished sales pitch about making a 20% down payment and getting a mortgage for the remaining 80% of the purchase price. But even when fully rented, the property still did not produce positive cash flow. When I asked why I should buy a property whose rental stream would not cover the mortgage payments plus taxes, he acted dumbfounded. Obviously, I did not recognize the "major opportunity" to purchase, and then subsidize from my own earnings, an asset which would inevitably go up in value driven by inflation. I passed, and the eventual buyer sustained a substantial loss on the property as inflation receded after several years and a considerable outlay of cash on his part.

---

* www.inflationdata.com. Accessed August 2011.
† www.forecastchart.com. Accessed August 2011.

And so, by the time Paul Volcker took over as chairman of the Federal Reserve Board in 1979, I had learned several important lessons.

First, I understood the basics of bond investing while most brokers at the time had no interest in bonds.

Second, I had had some success prospecting conservative, interest-earning savers who could become investors.

Finally, I had seen and lived through the inverted yield curve of the mid-1970s, so I recognized how rare it was to have short-term interest rates higher than the yield on longer-term, and thus riskier, bonds. (Long-term bonds are considered riskier than shorter-term bonds because more things can go wrong over the longer time period before their stated maturity date.)

To be sure, I was early in embracing what I saw as an interest rate opportunity of unparalleled proportions, and I sweated bullets as I called and talked to anyone who would listen about what I believed to be a once-in-a-lifetime opportunity. I put those convictions in writing and advertised them as best as I was legally allowed to do. Also, I committed every last dime of cash I owned personally to my belief that the high-interest-rate train was leaving the station for good.

In a nutshell, I believed and communicated to others that we were likely headed back to an environment very much like the 1950s, when the United States had reasonably low interest rates, slow but steady economic growth, and low inflation. I had no idea how low rates would eventually go, but believed that if we got the direction right, the results would take care of themselves as well as those who had committed their capital to this expectation. Both personally and professionally, I rode this disinflation train for nearly twenty years, believing that we were not going to eliminate inflation but were simply moving to a lower inflation plateau. Thus, every interest-rate uptick, such as in 1984 and again in 1989, provided another opportunity to buy the highest quality, longer-dated bonds available and continue to ride the disinflationary train.

Now many years and dollars later, I have yet to experience an inverted yield curve that did not present a major opportunity for investors to extend out the yield curve to own longer-dated bonds.

Note that in a later chapter, we will discuss my view that the train ride to lower interest rates arrived in the station some time ago and that we are now likely perched on a precipice with a valley on each side—one valley, deflationary; the other, inflationary.

LESSONS FOR YOUR ROAD TO FINANCIAL INDEPENDENCE:

✓ Develop your own visionary mind-set.

✓ If and when you sense a long-term shift or a new megatrend developing, be ready and willing to commit to that opportunity early and with conviction like our 1980 interest rate scenario or maybe the 2008–2009 bank and housing meltdown. Remember Warren Buffet's advice to be greedy when others are fearful and fearful when others are greedy.

✓ Recognize that all coins are two-sided and that on the opposite side from a problem is likely an opportunity in waiting. Really major opportunities often are found in the most stressful environments by taking the unpopular position. Sometimes the actions you don't take are also important. I never understood the dot-com boom and missed it. The result was also missing the bust that followed that bubble.

Bond Yield Curve Illustrations

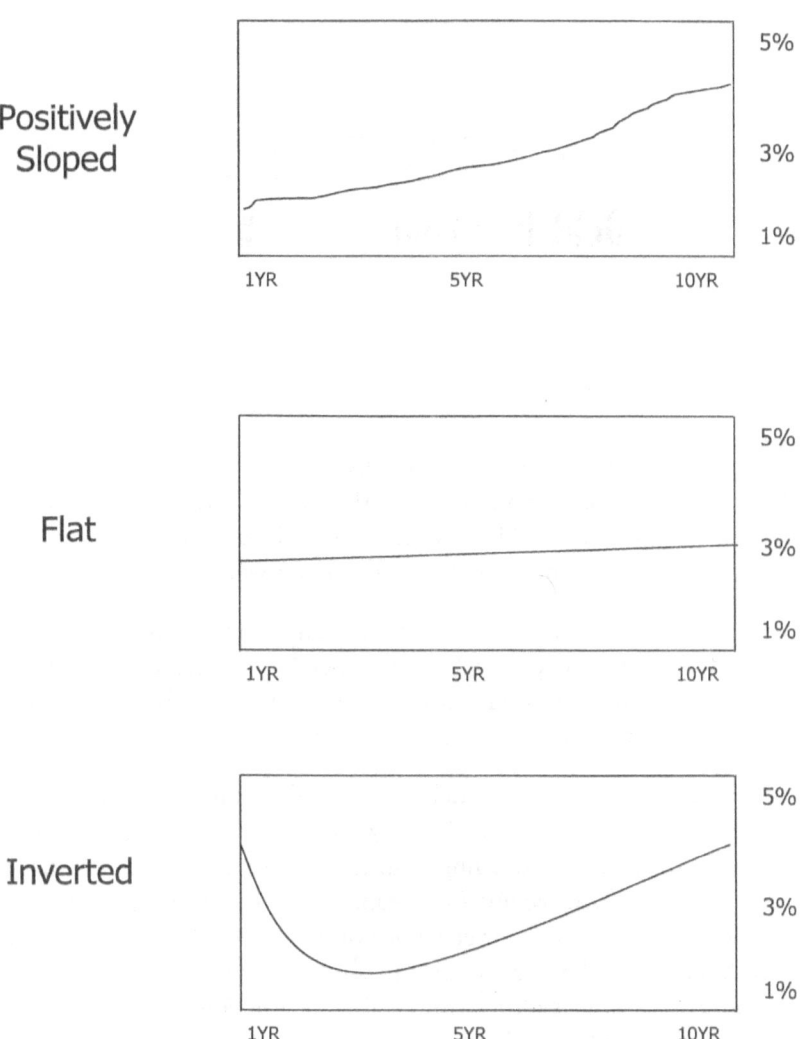

CHAPTER 6

Debt Is a Four-Letter Word

No doubt your parents, like mine, discouraged the use of four-letter words with the admonition that they were "dirty." So let me be crystal clear on this subject. I am absolutely convinced that when incurred for consumption, *debt* is a four-letter word.

Actually, I don't like debt of any type, although I can support incurring it for investment on occasion, but only when it is the result of a carefully researched business decision with no question as to the ability to service the debt under any potential economic scenario.

Some might say that our antidebt stance is almost un-American. After all, the average US household in early 2011 has something like $7,000 in credit card debt, and a huge number of personal residences have mortgages on them. Many Americans are so deeply in debt that in all likelihood, they will never be out of debt. Of course, some credit card holders pay off their accounts in total every month, and if so, that is fine. After all, it is almost impossible to function in today's world without the use of a credit card.

The target of our concern is the use of semipermanent, long-term debt to support the consumption of daily needs, because it can create an insurmountable obstacle to our personal financial independence. And unfortunately, a significant portion of our society gets caught in this trap. It is easy to do, readily available, and blatantly shoved at us in every conceivable way every day.

How can debt be avoided? It is not easy, and most of us are likely to incur some debt at various times in our lives. The biggest and best example is acquiring a mortgage to purchase a home. Rarely does a young or even not-so-young American have the financial resources to write a check and simply pay for his or her home. That said, we should not use this as an excuse to go out and pile on as much housing debt as we can possibly qualify for, or as we have seen in recent times, perhaps not legitimately qualify for.

For many years, our consumptive society has been driven by a "have it now; pay for it later" mentality. Soon we find ourselves in a situation where our stuff owns us.

Let's acknowledge that if we want to own a home or a condo, in most circumstances, we are likely to incur some debt. For this we recommend the following principles:

First, although it may take years to accumulate, save enough to make a substantial 20–30% down payment *and* limit the amount of your mortgage.

To accomplish this goal, don't buy the most expensive house you can possibly qualify for. Instead, reign in your appetite and hold down the total amount you will spend on housing.

Finally, accept the fact that a house is not a financial asset. That's correct; your house is not a financial asset. It is a place to live. Oh, I know. Some look at large impressive houses and assume they must be occupied by really wealthy people. Unfortunately, in a great many cases, it is simply a large house attached to a great deal of debt. And the owner may be the opposite of wealthy.

Since we have held this viewpoint for many years now, it did not come as a complete surprise to see the financial devastation visited on leveraged homeowners in the recent housing bubble implosion. But even so, we did not expect to see the extent to which it has occurred.

While a house that is under water when compared to its mortgage is a personal and now a national tragedy, it does not invalidate my view that one's house should not be considered a financial asset. First of all, houses consume money; they do not generate it. Even if you pay cash for yours, you must insure it, pay property taxes on it, maintain it, and repair it. That's what is meant by consuming money.

Of course, many may have planned to ride the wave of rising home prices to a point where they thought they could jump off with a big profit and live off that profit in the future. But that game is not a sure thing and never has been.

Many of the same arguments about avoiding debt for consumption can be made when purchasing an automobile. It begins to depreciate as soon as you drive it away and must also be insured, maintained, and repaired. We simply suggest buying within your means and avoiding debt, or at least, limiting the amount borrowed and the length of the loan.

We would add that leasing a car in appropriate circumstances can make sense if you approach it from the point of view that a car will cost you a certain dollar amount each month whether you lease it or save to buy it and then save to eventually replace it by paying cash again. If the terms are right, intelligent car leasing can make sense for someone who is truly dedicated to building their own net worth and does not want to tie up capital in a car. There is a case to be made on both sides of this argument.

Finally, let's turn to the subject of corporate debt or leverage. Financial leverage can be one of the most powerful forces in the world because, as its name implies, it levers the amount of money one can employ in a business, thus multiplying the amount of product that can be produced and sold. Of course, employing leverage is a two-way street. Because it requires timely interest and principal repayments, when the business cash flow slows, debt servicing can become difficult to sustain.

There is little doubt that corporate America has employed the use of debt to a growing extent over the past four decades. The result has been the potential for greater output as well as the potential for financial disaster. Today, we have witnessed the disaster scenario and are still in the midst of the fallout with the long-term ramifications still to be played out.

We grant that intelligent risk-taking, employed in well-thought-out corporate leveraging, can make sense in many situations. *We will, however, strongly contend that America has taken personal, corporate, and government leverage to a ridiculous level, and the ultimate cost is yet to be determined.* Investment banks employing 30-to-1 leverage left little room for error and helped set the stage for the financial implosion that has been the result.

The creation and use of the so-called shadow banking system and corporate off-balance-sheet financing played its part in levering up the risk/reward equation which had to lead to obscene riches or financial disaster eventually. At every level of American society, excessive debt has played a role in creating today's malaise and diminishing our children's future.

From the 1980s through 1995, lenders and investors collected real returns that allowed many to establish personal financial independence. But since then, the American tradition of pay-as-you-go in corporate and personal business practice continued to erode, resulting in the leveraging of America and much of the world, for that matter. Financial engineering became the hot game, and the players continued to roll their ever-more-leveraged dice until they rolled craps.

Right alongside this private sector leverage party, government entities expanded their balance sheets in unparalleled fashion. While we have had periods of sanity and even federal budgetary surpluses briefly in the 1990s, overall we would contend that since the so-called "war on poverty" of many years ago, Washington has fostered and rewarded a something-for-nothing mind-set which, like a cancer, has eaten away at our social and economic underpinnings. Today this problem has grown to a level where 75% of the 2011 federal budget is nondiscretionary and entitlement-based with the cumulative federal debt racing toward 100% of the GDP, a level many economists see as the economic tipping point.

Just as in the Great Depression of the 1930s, the federal government and the monetary authorities have been compelled to ride to the rescue to "save the system." At this juncture, the Fed's actions along with Washington fiscal policies and at least a partial private sector turn toward deleveraging have begun the process of reinflating the economic balloon. But the jury is still out on the eventual outcome and cost.

In the next chapter we will attempt to analyze further the issue of where we are and options for what we must do to survive and prosper. First, however, I would like to relay a real-life example of excessive debt that was seared into my brain at an early age.

You will recall my previous comments about my best friend, the young stockbroker. He came from a well-educated and successful East Coast family and was married to a young woman who was the daughter of a similarly successful, small-town community banker. Hers was a second-generation banking family, and her father and grandfather were still actively involved in their banking operations.

My friend was a very handsome young man who always made a great impression on anyone he met in a business or social setting. He had purchased a new home in a prosperous suburban community. Through family connections, he was able to obtain a substantial mortgage on that home. He also chose a vintage European sedan as his personal automobile. If you liked cars (and what red-blooded American boy did not), you had to love his. And from casual observation of his house, his car, and his impeccable suits, you could easily arrive at the conclusion that this young man was, indeed, eminently successful.

As a fashion side note, during my college days, a short six or seven years earlier, Cricketeer, an up-and-coming manufacturer of "natural-shoulder, Ivy League–styled suits," ran ads in the Wall Street Journal, featuring a dapper young male model. The caption read something like, "Cricketeer—for the man who wants to make $10,000 a year by the time he is 30." Well, my friend fit the look and the attitude of that model and no doubt had already exceeded the ad's income goal by the time we first met.

During the first year I was in the investment business, my friend called out of the blue, with a strong recommendation that I take a look at the over-the-counter stock of a small company that was in the computer leasing business. After very briefly describing what the company did, he concluded with the advice that I simply buy the stock and not look at it too closely. He said he knew that I was so conservative that if I looked too closely, I would never buy it.

He was right. I did look closely and decided not to invest or to recommend the stock to anyone I wanted to attract as a client.

Of course, computer leasing did become an exploding business, as what came to be known as electronic data processing was relatively new, and IBM and others were hard at work convincing every business that they could no longer operate efficiently without the power of computing in their arsenal.

I learned much later that in the months following our initial conversation, my friend had apparently talked everyone he knew, including his wife's family, into buying the stock of this wonder company. He personally bought on margin and further mortgaged his home to acquire more shares.

We talked only once or twice in the years that followed, and I confessed to him once that I had never invested in the company as it went from something like $6 per share to $60.

Several risk factors proved to be the unwinding of this tale of riches in the stock market. First, this was a very small company in an exploding business that had few barriers to new entrants. Second, my friend's investment portfolio was built on the unstable foundation of personal debt. Finally, because of his apparently insatiable appetite for driving the stock price higher, he and his clients more or less cornered the market for this company and had virtually no one to sell to once the bubble burst—which, of course, it finally did.

We learned about the ensuing personal and business tragedy in a phone conversation one weekend when our friend's spouse reluctantly told my wife that her husband had disappeared. Apparently, he had gotten on a plane to fly to New York to attend an investment conference and was never seen again. Of course, his family was devastated and left with a mountain of debts due to his failed investment strategy which was excessively leveraged and concentrated. Over time, because of their own personal wealth, his wife's family was able to absorb the various losses and move on. Several years of searching by private investigators only once turned up a trail as to his potential whereabouts, but to this day to the best of my knowledge, my old friend has never resurfaced.

Real stories like this can confirm our own views and values, or they can reshape us and head us on a different course. Perhaps you know of someone whose personal situation ended in similar tragedy.

LESSONS FOR YOUR ROAD TO FINANCIAL INDEPENDENCE:

- ✓ The use of leverage simply multiplies eventual outcomes be they positive or negative.

- ✓ Speculative borrowers know that eventually they might have to have a face-to-face conversation with their lenders which goes from "I have a problem" to "We have a problem." The current housing crisis is a prime example of this phenomenon.

- ✓ The interest meter runs 24/7 whether you are collecting interest or paying it.

- ✓ There is a major lesson relating to the multidecade American (and for that matter global) indulgence in the excessive use of credit. If you did not run with the crowd and lived within your means while pursuing your financial independence goal, when housing values collapsed so did your home's value but you had not used it as a piggy bank to draw down equity for expenditures and did not view your home as anything other than a place to live. Your net worth declined but your ability to support yourself likely did not take the same hit.

CHAPTER 7

Globalization and You

The use of the term *globalization* has become widespread over the years, but it has different meanings and nuances for each of us. There is one thing we can agree on, however. Our world has shrunk in the sense that we are not only American or British or Japanese citizens, but we are also citizens of the world. This shrinking phenomenon began back in the 1960s with the launching of the early communications satellites and has accelerated dramatically as the Internet has entered everyday life.

When the Internet investment bubble burst in 2000, and some related business entities imploded, there were literally thousands of miles of high-speed fiber-optic cable that were left dark and unused as a result of monumental overbuilding of data transmission capacity worldwide. True to the theory that no coin is so flat that it does not have two sides, this readily available capacity was slowly put to use in the years that followed for little or no cost. In turn, this enabled immense data flows around the world, accelerating the trend of being able to conduct business and transmit and receive vast amounts of information anywhere on the globe.

Also contributing to the spread of global business are worldwide democratization trends, as literally tens of millions of individuals have left the darkness of closed, dictatorial societies and entered into the sunlight of freedom and open political and economic environments. Suddenly cast upon the global stage as both producers and consumers, they represent one of the greatest megatrends of our lifetime, a human and economic tidal wave sweeping around the world with dozens of implications for social and economic systems and activities.

No doubt it will take years and likely decades for this wave with all of its attendant impacts to play out, giving birth or renewed meaning to terms like creative destruction, trade liberalization, political freedom, and supply chain management. What may have begun, at least symbolically, with the collapse of the Berlin Wall in the 1980s, still lives in the Middle Eastern and North African turmoil of 2011. Our goal is to find the investment opportunities herein.

Although we are each most closely affected by what happens in our own neighborhood, community, region, and country, we are also impacted, to a greater or lesser extent, by what happens in every corner of the globe—if not directly today then eventually, at least to some extent, tomorrow. These are the facts of life on planet Earth in the early twenty-first century, like it or not, so it does us little good to rant about it. Rather, it is in our self-interest to learn as much as we can about other peoples, cultures, and values so that we can make more informed and indeed relevant decisions about our own lives as we attempt to optimize our life outcomes.

It is also a fact of life that capital flows to enterprises and environments where maximum benefits can be realized by the deployment of that capital. Most capital today is truly global and owes no political allegiance to any flag or sovereign. This can put capital in distinct contrast to other traditional tools of economic activity, namely labor and resources or materials. Do not assume for a minute that we are referencing only private capital. It is likely that what are referred to as Sovereign Wealth funds are, at their core, capitalist pools of money, not simply political organizations—although no doubt the tug and pull of political versus business goals often clash within the management or investment committees of these financial giants.

As a result, some observers have advised that we should think globally but act locally, leaving us to draw our own conclusions as to how that actually plays out in our own lives and the lives of those around us.

✓ Globalization is the big megatrend of our age with all of its attendant risks and opportunities. It is dynamic and ever changing, but we need to exert our maximum effort to find both the big opportunities and risks to our financial well-being. Examples could be the inexorable rise in the demand for natural resources which will rise and fall with business cycles but would appear to be basically headed higher over the longer term. Energy, timber, potable water, metals, and agricultural products all could see huge demand growth in the years ahead with attendant investment opportunities attached.

✓ Globalization can optimize terms like *creative destruction* and *exploding possibilities.*

Chapter 8

Building Your Personal Financial Structure the Traditional Way

As a simple starting point, I have always found it useful to look at investments as two basic types—those that have guaranteed outcomes and those with uncertain outcomes.

Logically, any expected rate of return should be compared with what we believe is a sure thing. To illustrate: if we can buy a ten-year US government treasury note today at 2.0% and hold it until maturity, barring a default by the government, we can be assured of a 2.0% annual cash flow return for ten years. Accordingly, any other investment alternative we might consider needs to exceed this baseline return from what we deem as a safe asset and an assured result.

The difference between anticipated higher returns on lower credit quality bonds, or on stocks or real estate or farm ground or any other asset we could invest in, when compared to this baseline return, is referred to as the *spread*.

Simple logic dictates that if we have the option of collecting an assured 2.0% for ten years, anything else we evaluate on our investment comparison shopping list must have a higher expected rate of return to compensate for the additional risk we are taking with our invested capital.

Following this line of thinking, traditional investment portfolios are built from the ground up, starting with cash or equivalents as a base even though in most economic environments, readily available cash will earn the lowest rate of return (except for when the interest rate curve is inverted). Moving to the next step up the risk/reward staircase, we consider bonds of longer term and/or lower quality. Then we look at investments like stocks, which have no assured rate of return. Keep in mind that the difference between owning a bond and owning a stock can be defined as loaning (investing in debt) or owning (investing in equity).

Factors that cause bonds to fluctuate in value include changes in interest rates on competitive or identical issues and/or changes in credit quality. The general economic outlook and changing investor expectations about the future can also impact bond values. For example, owning an individual bond and holding it to maturity is one option, but owning an individual bond and expecting or needing to sell it before it matures creates a completely different set of risks. When we sell prior to maturity, we have no guarantee of the actual return we will earn and thus we become more like a stock or equity investor who enters into the investment venture with no assurances.

Over the years, we have built and managed hundreds of portfolios using traditional frameworks and methodologies with reasonable success. We refer to the process as *asset allocation*. The most widely referenced asset allocation resources we have used come from research that Ibbotson Associates produces and markets to investors and investment professionals. They provide both data charts and graphic illustrations which help nonprofessionals understand historical rates of return on various asset classes as well as on the range of returns for specific periods of time. Their work and that of other analysts show how the asset allocation process and various blends of asset categories have historically driven overall portfolio results. This can be useful in making allocation decisions for our investment assets with the caveat that historical data and results are not predictive of the future.

To recap, we recommend first comparing what we can earn from one investment that we believe to be assured to another with only hoped-for or expected returns, acknowledging that an investment's cash flow can often make a huge difference in its overall or total return over long periods of time.

After careful consideration of your financial situation and goals, we arrive at an asset allocation that we call our *strategic model*. This model is developed after we have accumulated enough cash for reserves to meet potential emergencies and can afford to put remaining cash to work in our long-term plan and portfolio for financial independence.

Let's assume that your hypothetical strategic asset allocation model simplistically calls for a 60% allocation to stocks and 40% to bonds based on both historical and anticipated levels of volatility and rates of return. Investment planning software systems can project this graphically for you and can indicate a range of potential outcomes and levels of volatility that might be experienced over a period of years. This exercise can prove invaluable in making sure that the shoe likely fits the wearer, meaning that based on past results, you can test-drive your portfolio and gain an understanding of potential outcomes.

To be sure, portfolio ranges of outcomes can have very wide variances, defined by what are called *standard deviations*. To illustrate, if a portfolio is projected to generate long-term average (mean) annual returns of say, 9.8% a year, approximately 66% of the time, it will have annual outcomes that range from a gain of 25.5% to a loss of 5.9%. This is called a one-standard-deviation variance from the statistical mean. A two-standard-deviation variance would cover 95% of probable annual outcomes and could fall within a range of plus 41.2% to minus 21.6% in any given year. A three-standard-deviation outcome would push the range of outcomes even wider, from plus 56.9% to minus 37.3% and cover 99% of probabilities. You can see these return ranges illustrated in the graph at the end of this chapter.

One of the benefits of this discussion and of your understanding of the concept is that it allows you to ask yourself, "Can I emotionally and financially stand a potential loss of let's say one standard deviation in a given year from our hypothetical portfolio?" Your answer to this question is critical. Although you may or may not know yourself well enough to give a totally honest answer, you absolutely must try. (The chart at the end of this chapter illustrates risks.)

And you must understand that if you live long enough, the odds greatly increase that you will live through a three-standard-deviation event (or one even more intense). In fact, if you were invested through the 2007–2009 financial crises, you lived through an almost four-standard-deviation financial market event! Having done so successfully, I would compare it to experiencing what seemed like a 20 on the financial Richter scale and living to tell about it.

Returning to the asset allocation process, what we described as our strategic asset allocation model generally needs to be rebalanced periodically. There are those who debate the need for monthly, quarterly, or annual rebalancing back to the original strategic levels, but I believe that rebalancing at least annually should be considered for most situations.

The need for rebalancing exists because, if left alone, over time the portfolio will take on completely different characteristics, and the risk/reward balance will shift accordingly. Look at various reports and charts from any number of sources that illustrate asset class performance year by year. You will often find that no matter which asset class was the best or worst performer one year, the results for the following year can be totally different. By rebalancing your portfolio, you can maintain an allocation that is appropriate for your situation rather than over- or underweighting last year's winner or loser.

Several other points are relevant before we leave the subject of asset allocation.

The easiest way to view traditional asset allocation is to select a blend of stocks, bonds, and cash that based on historic performance data is likely to provide a range of potential outcomes and volatility that you the investor can live with and that is likely to provide a mean or average rate of return that will meet your financial goals. That blend or asset mix will be your strategic blend and if you are committed to it, you need to annually rebalance back to that base mix by selling asset classes that have grown beyond the base allocation and buying asset classes that have underperformed. The logic that underpins this methodology is called *reversion to the mean*. In other words, if stocks outperform their historic mean, you subsequently expect them to underperform eventually, and you would therefore cut them back to your base allocation amount. You are selling some of the winners and buying more of the losers.

You can of course add the option of *tactical allocations* by intentionally choosing to strategically under- or overweight any asset class based on your forward-looking view not based on historic returns. Theoretically, today might provide just such an opportunity and environment, with the real inflation-adjusted yield on high-grade US bonds near zero and the stocks of large-dividend-paying companies selling in the lower range of historic price-to-earnings ratios. Tactical asset allocation decisions are obviously more sophisticated and subjective and thus can increase potential rewards, or in the alternative, result in portfolio underperformance.

There are research sources that attempt to project future or anticipated rates of return rather than supplying only historical rates of return. We have found this work to be a valuable addition to the information we use in designing portfolios, with the aforementioned caution applied.

In some cases, we make use of tactical asset allocation modeling which tends to be more flexible in times of economic volatility than the more static strategic allocation process, while relying on the strategic model as its base. A simple example might be that the overall strategic allocation-to-equities is 50%, but the tactician might employ a tactical range of 40% on the low side to 60% at the top. Of course, within the equity category, we normally use large-cap, mid-cap, small-cap, and international stocks, all of which could have both strategic and tactical allocations and ranges.

Tactical allocation decisions are generally made by projecting future expectations that vary from the past norms for a variety of reasons and are thus subjective in nature, requiring not only research and investigation but instinct and intuition.

A real-life example of taking a strong stance based on future expectations was referred to earlier when I referenced my own outsized bet that US inflation was going to be smashed in the early 1980s. As a result of that forward view, we dramatically overweighted long-term, high-quality, long-duration bonds at the expense of both stocks and cash to ride what we called the disinflation train. This illustrates the increased risks and/or rewards which can be leveraged by the tactical allocation decisions a portfolio manager or individual investor chooses to make.

While recognizing the risk in such an approach, I am convinced that tactical allocation decisions can make an enormous difference if projections of future outcomes prove to be timely and accurate. Many of these tactical allocation decisions can be very specific. For example, we are currently carrying a weighting of 10% in bonds denominated in currencies other than the US dollar which is twice our normal historical and strategic weighting for this asset category. This allocation worked fine in the recent past but has turned against us in recent months as the US dollar has rallied and our allocation is based on a long-term expectation for the dollar to decline in value against a number of emerging market currencies.

As an individual investor, you may or may not be able to successfully implement tactical asset allocations yourself, but I have on balance experienced good results in my own life and career.

We should also provide a brief overview of the *correlation of asset class returns*. For this discussion, we will assume that the US stock market—represented by the Standard & Poor's 500 stock index—our base "bogey," is assigned a factor of 1.0. The returns on all other asset classes can then be measured by the degree to which they mimic or track the S&P. If another asset class has an historical correlation of .95, we can expect a 95% correlation between its moves to those of the S&P. Therefore, we can assume it will have very little value in diversifying our portfolio because it is so similar. An example of this would be a portfolio composed of seven or eight investments, all of which are 90% or more correlated to our base. This would basically give us a handful of investments performing very much in line with each other and therefore not diversifying our overall portfolio to any meaningful degree.

Over the years there seems to have been more of a merging of asset correlations than existed many decades ago, as pointed out by several studies. Put another way, the opportunity for traditional diversification has narrowed. That does not mean we should abandon our diversification work. It simply means that we must be aware that the differentials have changed and may continue to change.

During extreme market conditions, such as the nearly four-standard-deviation washout in the most recent 2007–2009 financial markets collapse, differentials can nearly disappear altogether as correlations move toward 1.0, and the ability to create meaningful diversification is reduced.

LESSONS FOR YOUR ROAD TO FINANCIAL INDEPENDENCE:

✓ You don't necessarily have to be an investment expert or professional to succeed, but you do need a basic understanding of risk evaluation, outcome possibilities, and outcome variances.

✓ There is generally not much attention paid to the sequence of investment outcomes, but this is a critical factor for those seeking to retire. The decade since 2000, for example, has been one with several large market moves clustered into a relatively short time period of ten years. The most effective way to protect principal in this type of sequential situation is to build large cash balances to support planned spending before that spending is initiated after retirement. This cash cushion will thus prevent dipping into principal at inopportune times.

How About From A Diversified Portfolio Perspective?

The Normal Distribution

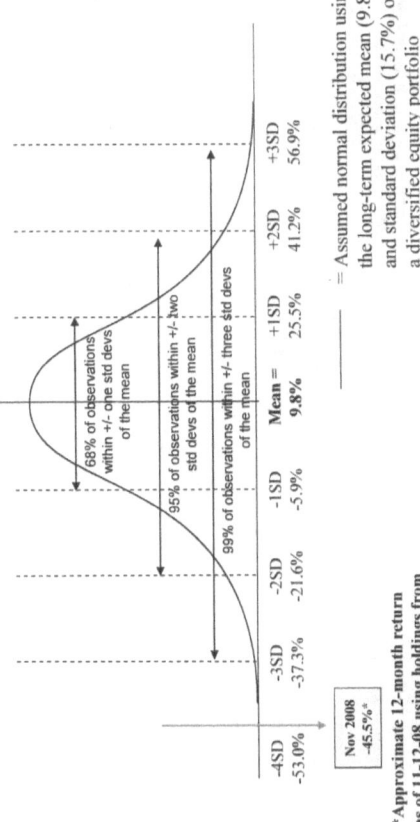

68% of observations within +/- one std devs of the mean

95% of observations within +/- two std devs of the mean

99% of observations within +/- three std devs of the mean

-4SD	-3SD	-2SD	-1SD	Mean =	+1SD	+2SD	+3SD
-53.0%	-37.3%	-21.6%	-5.9%	9.8%	25.5%	41.2%	56.9%

Nov 2008
-45.5%*

*Approximate 12-month return
as of 11-12-08 using holdings from
FactSet Research Systems, Inc.

—— = Assumed normal distribution using
the long-term expected mean (9.8%)
and standard deviation (15.7%) of
a diversified equity portfolio

Source: Mercer Investment Consulting, AMS Institutional Research

**Different story. Based on our expectations for a diversified portfolio, we are
experiencing close to a *negative four standard deviation event!***

RAYMOND JAMES
ASSET MANAGEMENT SERVICES

How About From A Diversified Portfolio Perspective?

This information is for educational purposes and should not be construed as a recommendation of any security outside of a managed account.

Standard Deviation: The volatility, or uncertainty, of future returns is a key concept of risk. Standard deviation is a statistic used to measure the volatility of returns around the portfolio's average return. The smaller the standard deviation, the tighter the band of return observations around the average return resulting in less historical return variability. Whereas a higher standard deviation indicates greater uncertainty regarding future returns.

S&P 500
A broad-based measurement of changes in stock market conditions based on the average performance of 500 widely held common stocks. It consists of 400 industrial, 40 utility, 20 transportation, and 40 financial companies listed on US market exchanges (mostly NYSE issues). It is a capitalization-weighted index calculated on a total return basis with dividend reinvested. The S&P 500 represents about 75% of the NYSE market capitalization.

Dow Jones Industrial Average
The Dow Jones Industrial Average is a composite of 30 stocks spread among a wide variety of industries, such as financial services, technology, retail, entertainment and consumer goods. The index represents approximately 23.8% of the US market, and is price weighted (component weightings are affected by changes in the stocks' prices).

CHAPTER 9

Managing Your Personal Financial Structure—A Way Forward

Anyone who has managed money or advised clients for a long period of time has experienced many different investment environments. If we have grown in our knowledge and abilities along the way, I hope we will be better at the craft than if we have simply had the same or similar experiences repeated over and over.

Lessons learned with real money in real markets can be invaluable if applied realistically to real people's lives by a conscientious practitioner. Of course it is critical to truly understand that each of us is different, and we have varying appetites for risk and reward. We are also emotional creatures and can be even more emotional when it comes to our money. Successful investing is very much like golf in that the greatest obstacles often exist in the short dimensional space between our ears.

There are times when it is beneficial to be fearful, and there are times when it pays to be bold. So the trick is to understand when to let each emotion creep into our investment mind and when to lean against those feelings. It takes a truly gifted investor to develop deep conviction when running against the prevailing views in the marketplace and to commit money or withdraw money based on those convictions. We are not talking about betting the ranch on one throw of the dice, but rather following convictions and instincts arrived at through a deliberative process.

Remember that sticking to a basic asset allocation plan and strategy is recommended in nearly every instance, noting that there are an infinite number of varied individual plans in use. We do, however, believe in a definite process to drive that plan and will attempt to explain it now.

I know from my own experience that I am not comfortable investing money without a road map, which I call a *global macro view*. The process for creating it follows, but before sailing into this dissertation, I acknowledge that not every investor or for that matter advisor has a big-picture orientation or can develop or obtain such a view. I just happen to be married to this big macro top-down process of searching for opportunities and risks then seeking out specific (micro) actions to take, because it has often worked for me. Accordingly, if you are an individual investor, a student, or a financial professional, I respectfully just ask that you hear me out in describing this approach then please adopt, modify, or reject it as you see fit. So, here goes.

First, develop a forward-looking forecast for various economies, markets, and societies that is both top-down and global. *Top-down* means it is a view from thirty thousand feet, a satellite view of the world if you will. You are looking for big trends and events—macro stuff.

From this global macro view, drill down to specific or micro trends and factors that might affect your investments and your investment results. This leads first to specific themes, then to asset categories, and then to specific vehicles or techniques you might employ toward your stated goal of achieving financial independence.

What are some of the big macro trends you might spot from our satellite view?

One trend is that the populations of the United States, Japan, and the Euro zone are generally aging and not growing other than through immigration, so think about the economic implications.

Aging populations naturally need more health-care services and have a higher proportion of the nonworking within their population. Occupations like nursing, physical therapy, fitness and wellness instruction, and nutritional training are more in demand.

Secondly, the populations of the so-called emerging and developing countries, such as India, China, Mexico, and Brazil, are growing much more rapidly and from within. The populations of the largely frontier countries, such as sub-Saharan Africa and the Middle East, are bursting with younger populations, many of whom are unemployed or unemployable. The demand for infrastructure building in the emerging world is mind-boggling, and that puts upward pressure on the value of everything from cement and steel to energy and water. A rising standard of living and burgeoning middle class increases the demand for any number of consumer goods and of course for a better and more high-protein diet.

In addition, we can easily discern that many of the world's peoples live in abject poverty. Although some are industrious and hardworking, others are not or have limited or nonexistent resources at their disposal and thus face a cruel fate in this globally competitive world marketplace. Some societies or areas of the globe are also held back by what we refer to as almost medieval societal or religious practices that can minimize their abilities to fully participate as global economic citizens.

Overall, we can observe that to potentially meet the material needs of a growing world, its resources are likely to be stretched and stressed as never before, challenging us to find ways to maximize outputs while minimizing wasteful practices.

A top-down global analysis can also lead to the observation that financial prudence in the management of our affairs is as critical for nations and societies as it is for individuals. Failure to follow sound practices can, over time, risk the political and economic freedoms that we have enjoyed and may assume to be natural. We are not entitled. We must earn and justify what we have and want. If you accept this view, think through the current global financial stresses for potential outcomes, winners and losers.

One of today's principal economic facts that I believe will play a very large role in everyone's financial future is the excessive amount of debt that we have loaded onto our economic wagon, particularly here in the United States. I mentioned earlier a strong personal aversion to excessive consumer debt and particularly debt incurred for consumption, but I am very much concerned about our total national debt, exacerbated by the huge borrowing and deficits of the past few years, much of it to finance two wars and the rescue of the American financial system.

As this is a book about finance, I will not engage in a discussion about the merits or necessity for any of the borrowing and spending we would lump together as part of our debt problem. I have already expressed disdain for the excessive leverage applied to the big investment banks' balance sheets, ramped even further by the shadow banking system of off-balance-sheet antics. Nor will I spend much time on the need for the financial system rescue which was applied in the recent crisis. Rightly or wrongly, the federal government and the Federal Reserve stepped up to rescue the system and prevent a collapse and ensuing depression. Both the short-term and long-term consequences of these "too big to fail" actions will be debated for years to come, and the ultimate consequences are yet to play out.

I do, however, believe that bad behavior should have consequences for the perpetrators—which includes us collectively to some extent, and I believe that it both has and will.

As tempting as it is to pontificate about the Greeks or other so-called peripheral economies of the Euro zone and their reckless spending, commitment to unsustainable social programs, etc., the biblical warning to those who would be the first to cast stones should apply. As Americans, all of us should look in our collective mirror.

Directly to this point and for reference purposes only, a landmark piece entitled *USA Inc.* was released in early 2011. This groundbreaking research, created by Mary Meeker and her team at Kleiner Perkins in California, is basically a presentation of what the USA, *viewed as a corporation*, looks like. It reveals in stark but very understandable terms how deep is the hole that we as a society have dug, and how failure to bend the curve of entitlements and borrowing to finance them could prove disastrous. We have long admired Ms. Meeker from our days at Morgan Stanley, where she worked as an award-winning technology analyst before moving on to her present position with the renowned Kleiner organization, but we particularly applaud this latest work, which can help a broad cross section of us to cut through the smoke and mirrors to see what the United States looks like from the perspective of an owner/investor, which we as citizens surely are.

I leave it to you as a citizen and individual investor to review this material and draw your own conclusions. However, as you have no doubt already surmised, I do not believe that the outlook for the United States is particularly bright unless we find both the public and private courage and resolve to alter our current path. My life experiences have often shown American society to be innovative and adaptive like no other in history, and our history has often been marked by major change. While historically I have always maintained the perspective of a glass half full, my current view is restrained by the demographic realities we face and by creeping doubt about our ability to collectively alter the direction in which we are drifting. For the record, I want to be wrong about this trend and will do whatever I can to help reverse it.

And so we stand as citizens of the USA and of the world in 2011, facing the greatest financial dilemma of our generation, trying to analyze where we are and what we can do to protect ourselves and those we care about. We are also concerned about our country and cherish the beacon of hope that America has been for these many decades, wanting to perpetuate what is best about our country for our heirs and future generations.

Most immediately however, for our narrow and specific purposes as investors, you and I must analyze what possible steps we can take in pursuit of our personal goal of individual financial independence. That is our focus on a micro level, and we must address it, here and now.

It seems to me that the US federal government has at least three options for how to deal with what we will simply call the debt crisis. These three possible options are 1) to formally default on our federal debt, 2) to attempt to grow our way out, or 3) to inflate our way out.

I believe that for now our country, or at least the Fed, has chosen option three. The Fed chairman has publicly stated that a primary monetary policy goal is to move the inflation rate up from its current very low level as measured by the core CPI (consumer price index), which is the CPI minus food and energy. I suspect that our massive monetization efforts have not yet created much higher inflation, because the velocity of money remains very low, and the consumer is slowly deleveraging, partially offsetting the government's actions in the opposite direction. If and when velocity or the turnover of the money supply picks up, hang on.

I also am convinced that the broader public expectation of inflation seems to be growing. And based on past experience, I believe that these expectations can drive ensuing reality when it comes to inflation. In other words, with all other things being equal, if consumers expect more inflation, their expectations can drive their actions, creating a self-fulfilling prophecy. I hear every day from average citizens and clients that consumer inflation is, in fact, here (that view based primarily on rising food and energy prices).

To come to some necessary conclusions, I personally believe that the jury is still out on the eventual outcome. What the Fed is doing to purposefully nudge the CPI higher is intended to avoid the deflationary abyss that we all looked straight in the face during 2008 and 2009. I would liken it to a patient in intensive care being supported by all manner of drugs and equipment, which must eventually be withdrawn as the patient attempts to climb back to a more normal state.

I frankly picture our economic vehicle going down a very narrow roadway with a sharp drop-off to either side. The canyon on one side represents a deflationary abyss and the other, an inflationary swamp. No one wants either as our ultimate fate, and so a steady-as-she-goes order from the bridge seems appropriate for now as the powers that be choose growth plus inflation as the best road toward our future.

Meanwhile, we are in the midst of a gigantic civil debate about the balance of power in this country, and the sound and fury from this debate will no doubt become deafening. With the irreversible surge of baby boomer retirements now on the runway, coming as they are on the heels of a multiyear spending-and-borrowing surge seldom equaled, the importance of this debate has never been greater.

It is probably not much of a stretch to argue that this current debate is very critical to our collective future as fundamentally the discussion is about what kind of country we want to have and live in. The voices on each side can be shrill, divisive, and yes, extreme.

There is real resentment on several fronts, and I am troubled by some related factors in this scene. First of all, America is suffering from a large underclass which cuts across racial and ethnic groups, who are not full and contributing citizens. To be sure, there are always groups of people in any society who are not productive and contributing participants for a variety of reasons. However, if you accept the thesis that we are inexorably locked in a global competition with the rest of the world for the resources all of mankind needs to sustain both fundamental life and so-called advanced civilization, then you have to ask how much of a welfare load, for lack of a better term, our society can carry and still be competitive and successful. When we read about the teen school dropout rate or what are now multigenerational families of children born out of wedlock and living in single-adult (not necessarily single-parent) homes and relying on state-sponsored welfare payments, we are not optimistic.

When we are told, as I have been by employers who hire entry-level, semiskilled workers, that up to 75% of their job applicants cannot pass a drug screen test, we are not encouraged and in fact wonder at the collective and individual economic costs being borne by family members and society as a whole in supporting these noncontributing members.

If you believe that the United States was essentially built by immigrants who came here seeking freedom of choice and economic opportunity, you may worry that America may have lost our "secret sauce." Of course there were slackers and criminals in those immigrant waves. We do not want to romanticize our view that those huddled masses that yearned to be free were also entirely virtuous, but we realize that ambition and drive were the primary forces behind America's development. There was no real safety net or agency that simply issued checks and thereby enabled mass, nonproductive life patterns. It may be that the best thing you and I can do or continue to do to protect and grow our own prospects for financial independence is to live below our means, truly rationalize our spending habits and "necessities list," build cash for opportunistic deployment or simple security, insist that our children understand and comply with many of the worldviews expressed in this work, and finally be constantly alert for the inevitable personal and financial opportunities that exist in a stressed and highly liquid environment such as we see today.

Following our comments earlier about economic or social slackers, I would be remiss if I did not admit that I personally recoil at the thought of those in positions of power and/or privilege who squander their success in material excess beyond reason or use the power of their positions for improper purposes. I am not so naive as to believe that if only we were all good little girls and boys, the world would be just fine, for it is clearly not that simple. I do however believe that it is no more legitimate to live unproductively off the sweat and toil of others, when your own inappropriate life choices have enabled you to exploit our system, than it is for those who have been materially or politically successful to overreach and abuse their positions for personal aggrandizement. We are each entitled to our personal life choices in the finest American tradition, but the messages that our personal lifestyle sends speaks to our true values and worth. Not speaking for anyone else, I have always appreciated great success worn humbly.

I have no intention here of attempting to predict ultimate economic outcomes other than to advise you to position yourself for our anticipated growth/inflation options, but monitor the game closely, and by all means employ a hedging strategy at the same time. Aiming at multiple targets is hard but probably necessary today. Some suggestions include the following:

✓ Expect general US dollar weakness against many other global currencies, especially the emerging countries which are major US trading partners, as the current crisis eases.

✓ Expect more general natural resource and commodity price increases but with potentially huge volatility. Longer term demand growth looks assured but with cyclical interruptions.

✓ Expect higher interest rates, especially in the United States, if the growth-with-inflation strategy is working. This will likely take some time to play out, if in fact a stronger recovery develops.

✓ Accept the risk of a Japanese-style economic stagnation in the United States if the government's strategy does not work as planned. This is the exact opposite of the above bullet point.

✓ Finally, position yourself to profit from the emerging world's consumers taking up the slack from a tapped-out and older Western consumer base.

There may appear to be some contradictions in this list, as we are not soothsayers who can accurately predict the future. The best I can do is gather data, develop observations based on that data, make judgments about possible future outcomes, and weigh the likelihood of those anticipated outcomes occurring. If there are outsized risks to our expectations or an unusually high degree of uncertainty (realizing uncertainty always exists in varied degrees), we can either temper our financial weightings or hedge them wherever possible.

Let's use one simple example of how this process might work. If you buy the thesis that the most dynamic source of future demand for consumer goods and services will come from emerging and developing countries, we can search for and invest in companies in those countries, if they are available, which might best meet those growing demands. On the other hand, we might choose to invest in Western-based global companies that sell into those developing markets. The difference might be that we do not want to run the political and/or economic or currency risks of buying into companies whose homes are in the emerging world but instead favor a more indirect route through more familiar names and vehicles. One potential negative in this simple example is, of course, that our result might be diluted from not investing directly so that we will not fully capture the growth of our target market. However, we are likely to have increased stability from these companies, whose major revenue is generated in more familiar and stable markets, accepting the fact that we are not achieving a direct emerging markets play and thus not maximizing our exposure to our target market.

If you buy into this top-down, global macro view of how investment themes can be discovered and developed, great. Of course, I realize that not everyone can or wants to do it, and there are some who, from a philosophical perspective, will argue that this is all just a waste of time. Critics of this process are entitled to their viewpoint, but I remain committed to this personal and professional process while acknowledging that it absolutely requires more intellectual searching and rigor than a more passive system might and does not ensure positive results.

With that brief introduction, let's discuss some of the options that we, as individual investors seeking individual financial independence, face when selecting a path to our destination. Specifically, we will consider the issue of choosing to be a passive or active investor, and secondly, whether to hire professional help or to be a self-directed investor.

Let's first discuss active-versus-passive portfolio investing. I have used each successfully and still do today in many portfolios. I am amused and sometimes saddened by the handful of financial columnists who seem to be obsessed by the mantra that index investing and incurring the lowest possible cost are solely responsible for the difference between success and failure in the investment world. Would that it were that simple! I would agree with critics that active asset managers cannot beat the indexes for their investment categories over long periods of times if they would grant that their simplistic view does not apply to all time periods in all asset categories. For example, simple *market capitalization-weighted indexing* in the large-cap equity space can reap rewards, but the same cannot always be said in the less efficient, small- and mid-cap equity markets, or in the below-investment grade, fixed income space, thus sometimes calling for the use of both active and passive vehicles and managers.

I also grimace when I read that what is referred to as *low-cost, index investing* is always the way to invest without any discussion about whether or not the writer is referring to equally weighted, market capitalization-weighted or value-weighted indexing or even understands the differences, which can be significant.

Finally, over the years, I have known a number of people who did a pretty decent job of managing their own money and making investment decisions. However, based on my experience, they are the exception, not the rule. Several asset management firms over the years have published data illustrating that over relatively long periods of time, while markets (or more specifically, market indexes) had an average annual return of, let's say, 8% for a decade, the typical investor over the same time period might have earned a 5% annualized return.

Why the difference? One answer is the old adage, "It's time in the market, not timing the market that gets results." Other obstacles we all face are the emotions of fear and greed.

Similarly, other research indicates that while Standard & Poor's 500 stock index from 1990 through 2010 returned a 9.14% average annual gain, missing or being out of the index for just the ten best days of that entire period would have caused the average annual return to fall to 4.08%. Missing the fifty best days of this twenty-year period would have actually resulted in a negative average annual result. (For reference, Capital Research—a major asset manager—has published data supportive of this conclusions within the past year or two.)

We present this data simply to illustrate a point: If you think that you can time your investments, good luck. Alternatively, if you believe that you have nerves of steel and can hold on to an investment that is plunging in value, you are indeed a rare individual. We refer you to our earlier discussion about having a strategic portfolio asset allocation model and following it. While I do believe in and allow for tactical changes and tactical ranges in an allocation blueprint, we also insist on rebalancing back toward, if not to, our strategic allocation. And I believe that tactical allocations are best made in anticipation of markets or trends, not in reaction to market volatility.

I believe that every individual investor should think through this process and at least mentally, if not actually, define his or her own strategic investment model.

In the end, my recommendation is to use the services of a professional advisor or planner to develop as well as manage this process, but I realize that not everyone will do that, and some will be able to make it successfully on their own.

One of the principal benefits of employing a professional is that they should have the training and resolve to work their system appropriately and keep you from turning right when you should turn left or keep you sitting still when you want to run. A really effective advisor knows the difference between left- and right-brained thinking and tendencies and should be able to effectively manage themselves and their clients. Can every advisor or planner do this well? Unfortunately, no, just as not every teacher or doctor or attorney can manage themselves, their process, or their clients effectively. That is why this relationship is so important and must be developed carefully and thoroughly. Both the client and the advisor have much to lose as well as much to gain from an effective business relationship and should develop both a frank and sensitive understanding of each other.

I have never been offended to realize that a prospective client was interviewing me just as I would advise a prospective client that I, too, want to know who is on the other side of the table and how well we might work together. It is important to understand whether or not we can communicate effectively and to determine if our expectations and understanding of our respective relationship responsibilities can be met. In any working relationship, communication, trust, knowledge, understanding, experience, and reputation are critical to success. In a business where sound judgment is essential, investing the time to develop the right relationship is time very well spent.

Successful investing over long periods of time and reaching the goal of individual financial independence is no proverbial walk in the park. If it were, the streets would be full of multimillionaires all singing as Sinatra did, "I did it my way." You can do it on your own, but you need to understand or find out how much intellectual and economic horsepower you have or can develop, how economically or financially intuitive or nonintuitive you are, whether you are at heart a saver or an investor, or whether you are a right-brained or left-brained thinker.

If you have to hire professional help to assist at several or all levels, by all means go about that task with the same vigor that your overall financial goal requires. If someone who is getting paid can hold you to your agreed course or insist that you modify your financial behavior or expose you to newer thinking and thereby increase your chances of successfully reaching your goal, more power to both of you and may you each prosper fairly and successfully, together.

LESSONS FOR YOUR ROAD TO FINANCIAL INDEPENDENCE:

✓ Significant investment experience does not assure results, but it can certainly help. If an individual does not feel up to the task alone, of course interview and hire a professional to guide you along the path.

✓ Developing a top-down global macro view and following it may be the best fit for today's dynamic global environment. I realize that this discussion is wide-ranging and challenging and that the times I am describing are very critical to our individual and collective futures. Accordingly, we need to devote all of our intellectual resources to our prospects and fully evaluate both our goals and our values.

✓ Real intellectual rigor applied here may well win out.

✓ Although specific suggestions and illustrations can be time sensitive and time can render them of little or no value, I urge you to accept and use the global macro word pictures in this chapter or modify them to fit your own outlook, as an example of the big picture critical observation process that I embrace.

✓ This is a key chapter presenting the author's current systemic preferences and beliefs. To gain the most from this wide-ranging discussion, try to apply the dialectic approach referred to in this book's introduction, by using the author's views as a thesis or proposition, your reactions to the proposed views and methodologies as an antithesis, and over time arrive at a conclusion or synthesis. This distillation process can be both fun and rewarding.

CHAPTER 10

Investing More Like an Institution and Less Like an Individual

The essence of investment management is the management of risks, not the management of returns.

—Benjamin Graham

You can observe a lot by just watching.

—Yogi Berra

There is little doubt that in recent years, many successful institutional investors have invested much differently than the majority of individual investors. To be sure, large institutions have a great deal more money to work with and can therefore hire more talent. That, however, is only part of the story.

One thing that differentiates these two worlds is the institutions' dedication to process. We have already stressed this concept, but want to again underscore the fact that successful institutional investors are committed to their investment process and either use consultants or hire internal staff to both develop and manage their investment process.

Another differentiator is that most institutional investors are not currently taxed on their investments. We are referring here to large educational endowments and major retirement plans, both public and private, as they do not face the obstacle of current taxation on their investment returns and thus have no reason to address this issue. Individual investors are in this position only when dealing with their own retirement plans, such 401(k)s, IRAs, etc.

Finally, we have the issue of sheer size which allows institutions to gain access to many investment vehicles, such as hedge funds, which can be purchased only by so-called "qualified" high-net-worth investors, or institutions which are considered experienced and sophisticated enough to analyze the risks they are taking. Many of the vehicles that institutions use fall into the so-called alternative investment category which is somewhat of a catch-all phrase used to describe a wide variety of vehicles or strategies.

Many institutional investors have much longer time horizons than do individuals, although as individual wealth expands, we encourage thinking well beyond just one person's or couple's lifetime. An institution typically expects to be in existence in perpetuity and so can think and act in multidecade time frames.

The fact that some institutions have earned much greater returns than many individuals over the past decade can be attributed in part to several or all of the aforementioned factors, but it is also true that many individuals have successfully adopted some of the best practices of institutions (such as their process) and have gained access to institutional-type investment options. The result is that a much broader base of investors are placing portions of their portfolios in often more complicated and sophisticated vehicles in an attempt to get in on the game, especially when it comes to nontraditional asset classes.

Some examples of these investments include funds of funds, commodity funds, long/short funds, hedge fund replication funds, and funds which can employ leverage or arbitrage techniques and short-selling activities. (Brief descriptions are on the following page.)

We caution that these are not mass-market products and that only more substantial, experienced, and qualified investors can and should consider them where appropriate.

But if they can be used appropriately in your pursuit of financial independence, then by all means investigate further. However, this could prove difficult as you will find that many financial advisors or planners may have very limited experience with or exposure to attractive alternative investments or strategies. Those who are experienced in this area likely deal primarily with high-net-worth investors, but even they may have somewhat limited understanding of investment products in this area. Accordingly, some investment firms have created alternative investment specialists or departments to conduct badly needed research and due diligence investigations.

When discussing nontraditional or alternative investments, it may help to understand their two main objectives. Some alternatives are designed to be *return enhancers* while others might be more appropriately viewed as *risk reducers*. We have prepared a simple one-page graphic below to illustrate the differences.

One of the vehicles I have used extensively with our clients, but only when and where appropriate, are funds of funds. I like the concept because the manager has the ability to employ any number of investment products within the overall host fund and thus can be very flexible and tactical in approach, all with total discretion. I do not know of a large number of them, but we have been very pleased with the very few we have used, and they are often either the core alternative or only true alternative investment I use in many portfolios.

I still use publicly traded *real estate investment trusts* or REITs. At times I have tactically committed as much as 10% of a portfolio to them, but our normal strategic allocation usually falls to only one-half that level. And while REITs used to have very low or even negative correlations to large-company stocks, that is now greatly narrowed, and their diversification value is thus not as great as in the past.

For appropriate clients with portfolios exceeding $1 million in value, I would consider using several alternative vehicles within the basic core portfolio or even creating a separate alternatives portfolio positioned as a satellite of the core. Such a *satellite alternative portfolio* could contain commodities, long/short market neutral, long/short with a long bias, managed futures, arbitrage, global macro, hedge funds, global fixed income/currencies, and global real estate investments.

The following are brief descriptions of various alternative investments.

✓ Global Macro—a strategy that bases holdings on broad macroeconomic and political trends

✓ Global Fixed Income/Currencies—invests in government and corporate bonds across the world; often not denominated in US dollars

✓ Global Real Estate—invests in real estate vehicles globally (can include the United States)

✓ Long/Short—this strategy buys equities it anticipates will go up in value while also selling equities it expects to decline in value

✓ Commodities—a physical asset, such as gold, silver, or oil

✓ Arbitrage—a strategy attempting to profit from perceived mispricing in the marketplace

✓ Hedge Fund (Replication)—seeks to provide a stream of returns similar to hedge funds without the accredited investor requirements or the high costs

✓ Managed Futures—trading focused on the futures markets

Return Enhancers

Core Investments

Risk Reducers

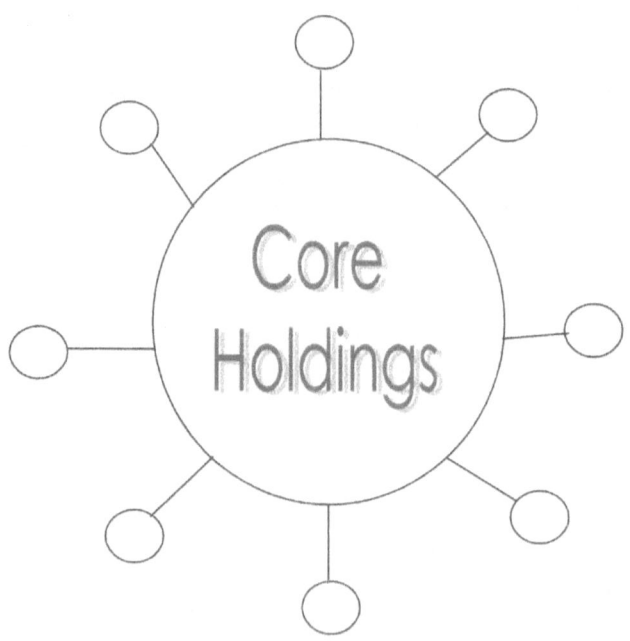

Core Holdings

Satellites

Finally, I want to spend a little time discussing the practice of hedging. *Hedging* basically involves investing in such a way as to help reduce the risk of adverse price movements in another investment. A simple example would be the use of *put* or *call options*. For example, if you own shares of a company and want to hedge that position, you could purchase a put option giving you the right to sell or put the stock to the option seller for a limited time and at a predetermined price. If the stock declines in value, the put may go up, partially offsetting the drop in the stock price. The stock might also stay the same or go up, and then the put option could expire worthless thus representing simply an "insurance" cost for this portfolio.

> *Note: Covered call writers are obligated to sell shares at the strike price if assigned, which limits possible gains and may result in a taxable gain for the option writer. This strategy does not usually provide protection from significant downward price movements and the covered call writer will not participate in any appreciation of the underlying stock above the strike price.*

> *A protective put hedge is a way to hedge potentially poor performance of a large holding. Put contracts give the holder the right to sell the underlying shares of stock at a predetermined strike price at or before a specified future date. While this places a definitive limit on any potential losses while preserving upside potential, the premiums associated with options can be expensive, contracts must be continually renewed, and the full cost of purchasing the protective put can be lost in a short period of time. This strategy raises the break-even price on the underlying security by the amount of the put premium.*

> *Options involve risk and are not suitable for all investors. When appropriate, options should comprise a modest portion of an investor's portfolio. Prior to buying or selling an option, a person must receive a copy of "Characteristics and Risks of Standardized Options" (ODD). Copies of the ODD are available from your financial advisor, Raymond James & Associates Inc., Member SIPC, at 217-431-0307 or from cboedirect.com/Resources/Intro.aspx.*

Hedging can also be accomplished by purchasing negatively correlated assets—in other words, assets which could go in the opposite direction of the security we are hedging, if we can find a truly negatively correlated asset.

A final hedging example, which we will discuss in more detail later, would be for the investor who holds a very large bond portfolio providing substantial cash flow, offset to a much smaller extent by some stock holdings with moderate long-term growth potential. One of the principal risks faced by an income-oriented investor is sharply higher future inflation which would likely drive up interest rates and thus drive bond prices down. In this situation, the income investor is faced with the need to hedge the risk to the value of his bond portfolio and can choose to do so by investing in vehicles which would be expected to move up in value in an inflationary environment. Typical examples of such investments could be commodities and natural resources, including energy. Broadly speaking, a hedging-and-diversification strategy could be appropriate in this particular instance, if one's view of the future calls for it.

We conclude this discussion about individual as compared with institutional investing with some data from the 2009 National Association of College and University Business Officers report, which indicates that the fifty-two university endowments in the United States managing more than $1 billion allocated an average of 61% of their portfolios to alternative asset classes in 2009. This figure compares to an allocation of 24.5% back in 1998 by the thirty-one university endowments that had over $1 billion under management at that time.

Thus the trend is clear for these entities, and at the very least calls for thoughtful consideration by appropriate individual investors who can now gain access to some comparable vehicles and strategies. While this suggestion is probably not appropriate for very small and/or beginning investors, it does apply to those who are much farther along the path to financial independence or have reached their goals and are now adopting more of a preservationist mind-set.

In the following chapters we will attempt to tie together some of these ideas and concepts in an effort to bring our various thoughts to some practical conclusions that you might use in your individual situation to assist in your pursuit of financial independence. Hopefully at the end of the day, you will have more insight and understanding of a broad process and systematic approach to investing.

LESSONS FOR YOUR ROAD TO FINANCIAL INDEPENDENCE:

✓ Seek out and use broader approaches to investing.

✓ Stay disciplined to your investment process but view it as evolving, not set in concrete.

✓ Beginning investors will find it difficult to do little more than build a basic stock, bond, and cash portfolio but need to be aware as their net worth and financial sophistication grows they may need to explore the world of alternative approaches and vehicles to more successfully manage their personal resources.

✓ It is not unusual for many alternative investments to be more costly than plain vanilla vehicles sometimes due to more than one level of management being employed or as with hedge funds, incentive payments for performance being paid to managers.

CHAPTER 11

Allocating Investments for Today's Bifurcated Worldview

Rather than provide a specific long-term guide as to what investments you should make, my purpose in writing this book is to give you an overview of the investment choices and challenges you face as an individual investor as well as a broad financial worldview that you may use to test your own expectations or outlook. In this process, I have shared some of my strongest forward-looking views and tried to present at least a glimpse of the investment process that I have developed and used over many years.

That said, at this point, I would like to share some specific current ideas as to how you might position assets based on my view that the financial world faces some starkly contrasted alternative outcomes.

Let's start by reviewing some previous points.

First, I believe that the USA has run the use of leverage to unsustainable levels. I do not know where the debt tipping point is, but I sense it could be close. If we surpass this point, we could face a downward spiral where debt controls us rather than the other way around. A picture of that financial whirlpool is truly frightening. Today, Greece is a frightening example of this debt and insolvency trap.

Similarly, I believe that America's obsession with housing over the past few decades has been excessive. I strongly believe that seeking a better home is part and parcel of seeking a better life and is one of our country's strongest values. That we should spend on housing only what we can truly afford and limit debt in this pursuit to a minimum, has not been a mainstream view.

Government policies that have promoted the pursuit of a single-family home for everyone are simply not realistic financially, considering that most of our population is overconcentrated in major metro areas which cannot geographically support this goal.

Another challenge to America remains a huge skills gap with many of our citizens not productively employable in today's global marketplace. If that percentage of the population grows sufficiently, just like the debt bubble, it can take control of our economic forces, potentially requiring too much of society's productive assets to support it with the result that overall productive capacity is restrained and thwarted.

Finally, as world population continues to explode, the entire globe faces the risk of diminishing resources. Many natural resources are indeed finite, and for some there is no adequate substitute, thus creating a challenge to both the availability of and access to these vital resources.

Assuming we accept their validity, how do we as individuals and as a nation address these macro factors, and how do we position ourselves for the future? Remember that we are raising these various macro economic issues and having this discussion in an attempt to identify trends that we can either exploit and profit from or downplay (maybe even avoid) to keep from getting in the path of a tidal wave that could swamp us financially.

As previously stated, I believe that the US government has decided to attempt to both grow and inflate our way out of our current economic challenges. I have also painted the opposite picture of a deflationary morass as a potential outcome.

You should probably position yourself for the possibility that one or the other of these outcomes will prevail, or alternatively hedge your bets and allocate resources, admitting that you are not willing to bet the ranch on one or the other eventuality, and try to cover both.

Let's refine this view a little by suggesting that if you are at the beginning of the process of building a financial portfolio, you might invest as though expecting the growth-with-inflation outcome. But at the same time, live your day-to-day life very conservatively to avoid being swamped if the deflationary outcome becomes the dominant scenario. Your goal would be to have cash to invest much later at pennies on the dollar compared with today's prices if deflation does occur. Specific investment allocations could include a large overweight to both emerging-markets equities and debt plus exposure to natural resources and commodities, offset with cash instead of what would normally be a conventional bond allocation.

If, on the other hand, you are well along in life and the financial-asset-building process, you might take a much more diversified posture, positioning assets in areas so some allocations should work out regardless of which side of the road the economic dice fall. The previous example of using emerging-markets equity and debt would also make sense here as would the natural resource and commodity plays. And an above-average dollop of cash could also be advisable, as would floating- or adjustable-rate bonds. You could add some high-grade, fixed income commitments but with the bonds underweighted compared to what you would allocate in a more stable or predictable environment.

You might consider investing in natural resources, including oil, natural gas and coal, basic minerals like copper and iron ore, rare earth metals, timber resources, and commodities in general. As of today, I believe that nearly every portfolio should contain exposure to these asset classes. Of course, which vehicles and how much vary widely from situation to situation, and no one size fits all.

I believe it is doubly important to seek dividend yields when investing in stocks because historically, dividends have provided a huge portion of their expected return and because in many portfolios, we are recommending an underweight to what would be a normal bond allocation. This underallocation to bonds makes it imperative that other portfolio assets throw off cash, especially if the investor needs cash flow for living expenses.

Subject to future change, one of my current favorite ways to address the need for cash flow and hedge against rising inflation as well as the steadily growing demand for energy is through the use of *master limited partnerships* (MLPs). Most of the companies that own and operate many of the nation's oil and gas pipelines and energy storage facilities are structured as MLPs. Through their favored tax structures, they serve as flow-through investment vehicles. Similar to the real estate investment trust (REIT) industry, these companies do not pay taxes on current income, but instead flow their income and accompanying tax liability on to the investor. In today's marketplace, cash distributions of 6% or more are common for energy MLPs, and historically those distributions have tended to grow slowly over time, although there is no assurance that trend will continue. We look at them as providing inflation-hedged income streams which fit well with the themes referenced here so they could be appropriate for older or conservative income-oriented investors wanting a check in the mailbox or those who are not yet using investment income to live on but are concerned about the future impact of inflation.

A word of caution exists because owning energy MLPs will result in the issuance of K-1 tax reports rather than 1099s. As some of the distributions can be classified as unrelated business income (UBTI) if received inside a qualified retirement or other tax-exempt plan, you are probably well advised to not purchase MLPs directly within a qualified retirement plan. You can, however, use closed-end or exchange-traded funds that own MLPs but issue 1099s to their shareholders rather than K-1s, thus avoiding the aforementioned tax situation. Because of the potentially complex tax issues involved when investing in this area, I would recommend obtaining preinvestment tax advice.

Finally, I would reiterate my commitment to alternative vehicles and strategies which may reduce risks and/or improve returns. At a minimum, I favor some funds of funds, especially those managed by the most sophisticated managers who are well versed in this arena and have the intellectual horsepower to manage such a strategy effectively.

Alternative investment approaches are called for, as I strongly believe that right now in 2011, we are in a much different place than we have seen before.

I have been incredibly fortunate to have inherited a strong work ethic, and to have developed a love for seeking out large global trends as a result of having an internal big-picture orientation. Perhaps your mind works differently, and no doubt it does. Perhaps, like me, you see or will see in your life one (or more) big, long-wave opportunity, and you will pursue it. Having become convinced early that several decades of inflation-ridden cycles were ending and that a long-term interest rate train was pulling out on a one-way trip to a new future has turned out to be my personal opportunity of a lifetime.

It is possible that today one of those long-wave opportunities is staring right at us waiting for discovery. Some of the work being done in biotechnology, for example, could literally bear life-altering outcomes, and some small biotech company could become a major pharmaceutical player. Additionally, potential alternative energy options could be developed that might allow us to stretch our current resources far beyond what appears to be likely today and at an economically viable cost, which so far does not seem apparent to me. The development of horizontal drilling techniques has certainly changed the availability of US natural gas in a mind-boggling fashion in the past few years.

Consider that some resources are no doubt going to be challenged. One example is the availability of prime topsoil for growing grains, as US topsoil levels continue to diminish while Brazil and several other countries still have huge crop production potential. Couple this with the possibility that the use of effective pesticides and fertilizers is limited, and you see the challenges and potential opportunities to produce an adequate future food supply, especially one built on a surging global middle class intent on consuming more animal protein. No wonder Midwestern farm values have surged to previously unimagined levels recently. Could the same surge eventually occur in prime US timberlands now depressed by the collapse of new home building?

If we in America can preserve the spirit and entrepreneurial drive that built the world's productive capacity, we have a bright future. It is absolutely essential to our collective and individual futures that we honor and encourage innovation and questioning as well as the goal of economic or financial independence. An informed and committed citizenry is vital and best nourished by each of us individually taking up the challenge for ourselves, knowing that we maximize our ability to survive together if we succeed individually. This book is a short attempt to reveal a number of large important economic and social issues that you and I need to be aware of and decide if and how they will impact us and the financial security of our families.

Much of this conversation is heavy and can be depressing if viewed strictly from the context of the immediate problem, but some of it, if seen through the eyes of an opportunistic entrepreneur, is a major opportunity to profit personally and advance society generally by remembering that often one man's problem is another man's opportunity. Finally, it is a shame that many in the political arena either fail to recognize this economic reality or prefer to demagogue issues for political gains by playing to the baser jealousy factors that some constituents harbor.

LESSONS FOR YOUR ROAD TO FINANCIAL INDEPENDENCE:

✓ Today your portfolio probably needs to be aimed at more than one potential environment and multiple outcome scenarios. This is much harder to do then the old standard approaches to investing, but it is a reality of our current situation that some accurately refer to as the new normal. After all, if we face potential multiple outcomes that are radically different, we may just need a radically altered approach coupled with a great deal more flexibility than previously thought necessary.

✓ Learn to play "what if" and imagine future outcomes and possibilities. Read about and study how a visionary mind works to break through the mental cobwebs which might exist in our minds. Make sure that you are looking at the future through your mind's windshield and not into the rearview mirror, mistaking it for what is coming at you.

A visionary mind sees things as they might or could be, not just as they are today. An activist visionary is inclined to attempt to shape outcomes rather than be shaped by them.

A Traditionally Balanced Portfolio Allocation
May 2011

Cash	4%
Domestic high-grade bonds	20%
Global bonds (not US$ hedged)	10%
High yield bonds	5%
Emerging market equities	5%
Small-cap equities	5%
Mid-cap equities	5%
Global large-cap equities	11%
Large-cap value*	10%
Large-cap growth*	10%
REITS and MLPs	5%
Fund of Funds	10%

*Because many large-cap domestically based companies are global in nature, actual exposure to international markets becomes greater than may be implied or indicated by this allocation matrix. Generally speaking, a global manager may invest anywhere, including the United States, while an international manager would invest outside of the United States.

A Hypothetical Portfolio Configuration for an Established High-Net-Worth Individual Investor May 2011

This is an example of a multiportfolio configuration you might find in use by a high-net-worth investor who has been investing for years and has more or less acquired sufficient assets to meet her financially independent benchmark.

PORTFOLIO #1

This large portfolio consists almost exclusively of high-grade municipal and a few taxable corporate, government, or international bonds that provide current cash flow which can be reinvested while not needed or partially used as a current income source. Obviously this portfolio has been built by aggressive after-tax savings generally over a long period of years.

PORTFOLIO #2

This portfolio consists of qualified retirement plan assets, such as 401(k), 403(b), or SEP and IRA assets. Accordingly these assets are currently tax sheltered and tax deferred. The portfolio would generally be a balanced growth and income portfolio with growth emphasized more. Other than assets rolled over from other qualified plans, these portfolios have been accumulated with pretax contributions through payroll withholding elections or earned, taxed, and then contributed as tax deductible contributions in the case of contributory IRAs, etc. If employer-sponsored plans prevail herein, participants are generally restricted to investing in a limited number of vehicles with accompanying limitations on diversification possibilities.

PORTFOLIO #3

This portfolio could be constructed as a satellite alternative asset portfolio and be funded with after-tax savings and generally not used to provide for current income needs, although that is an individual choice.

In this portfolio which in all likelihood was the last bucket of money to be funded, we would generally find the most nontraditional assets. This portfolio would thus not be a carbon copy of either of the first two portfolios but instead would likely contain assets or investment styles that are intended to both enhance returns and diminish risk. Accordingly, the entire cornucopia of alternative strategies might be employed from long/short or hedge fund replication vehicles to commodities, real estate, and natural resources. This is usually the most sophisticated of the three money pools used in this example and is often constructed with the expectation that it will in many cases perform somewhere between the return on broad stock and bond market averages.

This three-portfolio concept can exist because practically it might represent what is possible and likely to occur over the working lifetime of a committed saver. Conversely it is highly unlikely that a younger or beginning investor would have this portfolio configuration. Coincidentally, there can be an unintended advantage to this configuration because it will be possible to have differentiated investment policies for each portfolio and to measure performance of each separate bucket of money as well as the performance of the three aggregated portfolios.

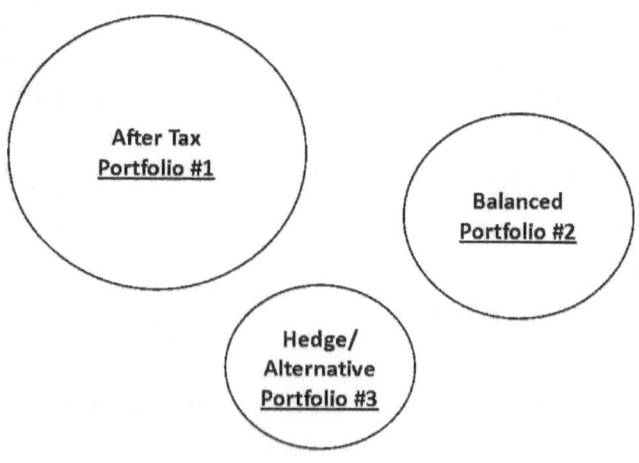

CHAPTER 12

What Role Does Life Insurance Play in Your Game Plan?

We have chosen to address the subject of life insurance because of the role it has played in the financial lives of many, if not most, middle-class Americans. Therefore, we begin this very basic survey by describing our view that traditionally, life insurance products have had two parts to them. The first is an actuarially determined cost to protect against the possibility of the premature death of the insured. The second part of the traditional insurance contract is the savings or investment portion. If your life insurance contract had both protection and a cash value account, it was said to be a permanent or whole life policy.

Over the years, the insurance industry has been very innovative, creating various life products where the cash value portion of the contract has become an investment vehicle much like mutual funds, in place of what we would have referred to as fixed or backed by the general account of the insurance company. In traditional *whole life insurance*, the investment risk resides with the insurance company whereas in today's variable life products, the investment risk resides with the policy owner, not the insurance company. The same risk transfer from the company to the insured exists in what are called universal variable life contracts. This is a very distinct and basic difference, and it requires a much more sophisticated policy owner to make and monitor investment selections.

Continuing with the traditional choices the public faced when deciding if life insurance protection was indeed called for, the other option available was and is what the industry calls *term insurance*. Term policies provide a death benefit, period. The insurance company calculates the risk of premature death given specific parameters, such as age and health, and charges accordingly, so the person buying a term policy is buying only a future death benefit or protection.

The differences between a whole life insurance contract and a term policy are considerable. The only benefit ever to be gained from a term policy will be the payment in the event of the death of the insured during the specific term of the policy. The whole life contract also pays at the death of the insured but has a cash value that can build along the way, as well. That said, how does the investor who is driven to become financially independent make a decision between the two, if he or she has determined that a death benefit is needed?

Stepping back for a moment, a competent planner, advisor, or agent can assist in quantifying the amount of death benefit that could be required should you not live a normal life span. This process is arrived at by calculating the costs of retiring a home mortgage, educating minor children, paying off final expenses, etc., and coming up with a payoff or protection number.

Obviously, the decision is critical because it is not unusual for a young adult with a family to have a great unmet financial need in the event of an untimely demise while at the same time perhaps having limited ability to pay for that protection. In fact, it is often the case that you will face the option of either buying an inadequate amount of whole life protection up to the point where you are just not able to pay for more, or buying a much larger and thus more adequate amount of pure term death benefit for the same or similar cost. If this is an accurate description of a typical life insurance decision, then why would anyone chose the higher cost product with not enough death benefit to address unmet needs?

Our response is that before you step into what appears to be the obviously intelligent choice, you need to know if you are truly a saver or a spender. Why does this matter? While term costs will be much lower per thousand dollars of death benefit for a healthy young adult, it is imperative that this same young adult be committed to the pursuit of financial independence and that he or she succeed in this quest. If you are not a big-time saver, you will eventually have to face the fact that the cost of pure term protection will grow as you age, eventually reaching the point of being unaffordable. On the other hand, looking back to the pie chart in chapter 2 on financial choices, we can see that, for a committed saver and investor, this protection is an expense to incur while saving aggressively and until we no longer need the death benefit, because we have reached our financial goal and accumulated sufficient assets to cover the various financial needs mentioned previously.

So where does this leave us regarding life insurance? It leaves us with a quandary, because as we have pointed out, the average American is a spender, not a saver, and that creates a challenge when it comes to the subject of life insurance decisions. We might have to conclude that if we are not so committed to our own financial future, that we can be that dedicated saver, we and our heirs will simply have to pay the price of needing an insurance company to take money away from us through whole life premiums and return a portion of that premium to us over time to make up for our lack of financial discipline. This does not make us a bad person. It simply means that someone else needs to save for us because we will not do it on our own.

My personal choice was to always buy term so that I could get the most death benefit protection for the lowest dollar outlay and keep my saving and investing function completely separate. I realize that choice was the right one for me but not for everyone, and so be it.

Here are a few final thoughts regarding whole life, cash value, and death benefits. The *death benefit* is what is paid at the death of the insured, while the *cash value* in a whole life policy remains with the insurance company at the insured's death. Alternatively the so-called dividends which create the cash value in a whole life policy can be used to purchase additional death benefits, but the forced savings we referred to earlier are thus not available for a living benefit. Alternatively, the cash value can be borrowed or withdrawn from a whole life policy for current, or what we might call living needs as opposed to death benefit. If, at the time of death, a loan exists against the policy, it will be repaid to the insurance company out of the death benefit. In addition, any loans or withdrawals should be thoroughly reviewed with one's tax advisor and insurance agent.

As a footnote to our discussion of life insurance, if we are very successful investors and amass enough personal wealth by the end of our lives to create the potential for substantial estate taxes, life insurance can be effectively used to offset that tax bill. In this situation, we would first create an *irrevocable life insurance trust* (referred to as an ILIT). Then, with annual gifting to the ILIT, its trustee can purchase a life insurance contract outside of and separate from the taxable estate of the insured in order to offset the expected tax burden at death. Careful document drafting and competent estate planning advice is required in these cases, but where appropriate, affordable, and desired, this estate planning tool for the wealthy can be an effective means to help offset potential estate taxes.

LESSON FOR YOUR ROAD TO FINANCIAL INDEPENDENCE:

✓ Life insurance can be a difficult and jargon-laden mine field for most individuals, so take your time and keep it basic.

CHAPTER 13

Other Estate and Financial
Planning Techniques*

Although most of us have some type of system for keeping track of our financial lives, some are much more accurate, current, and useful than others. Suffice it to say that simply stuffing financial statements or records into file folders is not sufficient. Creating a family planning notebook is something I always recommend to clients.

You might start with a three-ring binder which is organized into various sections containing basic information about what you have and where it is. In the front should be a contents page which lists and numbers the various sections, including retirement plans, life insurance, other insurance, banking relationships and accounts, CPA name and contact

---

*   Although the author is a graduate of the American College Estate Planning for Professionals certificate program and a longtime experienced financial advisor, the materials contained herein should be viewed as for discussion purposes only and not relied upon when making actual estate planning decisions. Such decisions should only be made after review by one's own tax and legal advisors. Accompanying tables can illustrate both annual and lifetime gifting limits which are of course always subject to changes.

information, attorney name and contact information, investment accounts and locations, real estate, etc.

Give some thought to writing a family legacy statement about yourself, your life, and your values. I have taken the time to do this and have shared it with my spouse and grown children so that they know what our family owns and what we stand for as a family unit. You might find this to be a valuable exercise, but do not underestimate the difficulty you may face in pulling together all of your thoughts.

Finally, keep your family planning book in a place that is accessible to your next-of-kin or executor, and give your spouse and children their own copy. If, perhaps, you are hesitant to provide complete financial information to your children, you could give them a copy with basic reference pages and information about each section while leaving out actual numbers.

Of course everyone needs a last will and testament plus basic *financial and health-care powers of attorney*. While many states provide prototype durable POAs to guide you in this process, I recommend that you have an attorney draft your documents.

Over the years I have strongly recommended the use of a *revocable living trust* as a basic estate document. I established living trusts for myself and my spouse in the early 1990s. There are many benefits to having such a trust, not the least of which is the fact that it is revocable and, as the maker or grantor of the trust, you can amend or terminate it at any time. You can act as your own trustee and therefore make all of the investment and other decisions for your trust just as you always have.

In addition to acting as your own trustee, you can choose to name someone else or a professional or corporate trust company to act for you. Obviously, you will want a competent and trusted successor trustee who will step in when you are no longer alive or able to act on your own behalf. Over the years, I have witnessed several very painful situations when individuals have declined over time to the point that they no longer had the mental capacity to act for themselves, but they did not have appropriate documents or procedures in place to handle this challenge. I believe it is terribly unfair to yourself and everyone else to postpone decisions like estate planning, the selection of successor trustees or attorneys-in-fact, and other vital decisions, until you are sick or under similar duress. Make these planning decisions when you are under absolutely no pressure to do so, execute what is needed, and then go on and live your life, knowing that you have addressed your personal financial business rationally. You do not want to undertake this process because you suddenly face a potentially deadly illness or are told by family or friends that you might be "losing it" mentally.

It is important that you not only create your living trust but that you also fund it by retitling various financial and other assets into the official name of your trust. Failure to fund the trust means that you have not actually accomplished anything and leaves your estate as it was before. When a revocable living trust is your basic estate document, it is normally accompanied by what estate attorneys refer to as a "pour-over will," which could be used in the event that some item might have been missed in the retitling process.

Taking these steps enables your successor to take over either permanently or temporarily in the event of your inability to act. It contains specific language which describes how incompetency is to be determined privately rather than by the courts.

At the time of your death, your trust becomes irrevocable, and your successor trustee steps in to carry out the exact disposition of your trust assets as you have outlined in your document. This final process is carried out privately without the supervision of a probate court and without your estate becoming a matter of public record.

Your trust assets can be distributed in whole or in part at that time, or the trust can stay in existence for the future (income) benefit of your heirs. Depending on the size of your estate and prevailing estate tax laws, the original trust could be divided into two trust entities at your death, again with the administration of professional tax and legal counsel.

There are other estate-related issues that you may want to address during your lifetime.

The first involves the careful planning for the beneficiary or beneficiaries of your retirement plan or *IRA*. Many large IRA portfolios that were rolled over from previous employer-sponsored retirement plans may require the careful planning referenced here. For example, a surviving spouse who is named as your beneficiary can roll over your IRA to his or her own. They can also roll over to a beneficiary IRA as can nonspousal beneficiaries, carefully following the current tax regulations about future required distributions. These are sometimes referred to as *stretch IRAs*, as they stretch or extend the income and thus tax impact over time. Of course, such decisions should be made only under the direction of competent tax counsel.

You can also consider charitable gifts which might be made during your lifetime or at your death and also come under the estate-planning banner. Examples of planning techniques in this arena could include gifts to charities from an IRA directly to the charity to avoid income tax liability on that money. The value of such bequests is still included in your gross estate, however, when calculating any federal estate tax liability.

For gifting during your lifetime, you might consider creating a *charitable remainder trust* (CRT) and funding it with very highly appreciated stock or other property which, if sold outside a charitable trust, would incur capital gains taxes. I have effectively recommended this approach to individuals who have large concentrations of personal wealth in the stock of one company and need to prudently diversify that asset but are concerned about the adverse tax consequences. By creating and funding a CRT with this asset, they can subsequently have the trustee of the CRT sell and diversify the proceeds while taking advantage of a current income tax charitable deduction and retaining a lifetime income stream from the trust assets. Of course one must have true charitable intent in taking this action as no amount of tax savings will completely recoup the value of the donated asset. These decisions should be thoroughly discussed and planned with the assistance of your estate and tax counsel.

Finally, we come to the subject of *gifting*. You can make lifetime gifts to anyone each year, taking advantage of the annual gift tax exclusion allowance. You can also make a onetime gift. Such gifting can be used to assist your children or grandchildren or others over time and to reduce a potentially taxable estate. It can also provide the experience of letting your heirs "test-drive," so to speak, enabling you to see exactly how they react to and handle such financial gifts. After all, the purpose of most gifting is to assist someone else but not turn them into a financial dependent or enable some undesirable behavior.

LESSONS FOR YOUR ROAD TO FINANCIAL INDEPENDENCE:

✓ Get organized, put it in writing, and give the information to appropriate heirs.

✓ Find and employ an experienced estate planner or estate planning attorney.

CHAPTER 14

Gifting

A gift is something that is bestowed voluntarily and without compensation.

Almost everyone sometime in life freely elects to make a financial gift to another person or organization. This can be the simple birthday check to a child or grandchild or something more substantial.

My life experience teaches me that gifting is a marvelous opportunity to show gratitude to someone or something, but it can also be both a learning and a teaching tool.

We have already communicated our belief that individuals have a tendency to be either a spender or a saver at heart, and gifting can be an indicator of one's tendencies in this regard.

Personal thrift can be taught by a parent or grandparent to any child very early in life with simple gifting and saving lessons. Many a child has a piggy bank into which they regularly save by depositing their coins. Sometimes what we have referred to as "the saving thing" comes naturally and sometimes not, but assuming that it can be taught, helping a child create the habit of saving could reward them for their entire lifetime. We recognize that some people are almost automatically turned off by this concept, instinctively insisting that this simply encourages hording or greed. However, we believe that the "live for today and to hell with tomorrow" mind-set misses the entire point of learning to use money as a tool for a better and more secure life experience.

Any child who has been taught simple thrift and the saving habit early in life will have a real advantage over those not lucky enough to have learned this skill. The saving habit begins a lifetime journey for both the giver and the receiver of the gifted item, for once learned and put into practice, you can leverage your life to another level. By this we simply mean that you will no doubt have opportunities to employ what you have materially accumulated for your own growth and enjoyment, but you will also be able to leverage your values and gift to a level that will help fund individuals and organizations, enabling them to contribute to a better world for all.

Regular and systematic gifting within one's means can be practiced throughout a lifetime, and yes, it can be perpetuated. Typical examples of gifting are annual gifts to churches, to community fund drives (such as the United Way), and to other favorite organizations, and we heartily encourage and have always participated in these activities. However, you might also consider gifting to children and grandchildren, not just for the purpose of being supportive or generous, but also with a secondary purpose of finding out how they react and handle such gifts.

Make no mistake here—a gift is a gift, freely given and without strings attached, and that is as it should be. However, it is my experience that if you really want to find out what someone is like, give them money.

Money can remove inhibitions and may result in reckless, even self-destructive, spending. There are many examples of excessive wealth leading to self-destructive behavior, and they are not only ugly but sometimes are public or private tragedies.

Admittedly most of us think that we will never accumulate enough worldly wealth to ever gift to someone else and thereby release that recipient's destructive inhibitions, but that is not necessarily true. We have seen people of moderate means, for example, pay off five- and even six-figure credit card debt racked up by a freely spending adult child with no strings attached, and the same thing done with the insistence that a repayment schedule be recorded and honored by the miscreant spender. We choose not to put either a good or bad label on either of these actions but instead to simply illustrate real-life examples of gifting and consequences.

We have been privileged to see mature adult children who have received annual gifts and used them to save for a major purchase or need, demonstrating maturity, self-control, and commitment to long-term goals. These demonstrations deserve consideration when making future lifetime and estate gifts. Our oldest grandchild, now an accomplished pianist, plays and practices on his family's grand piano, purchased in part from accumulated gifts saved over several years by his parents who could have used that money for immediate consumption but instead chose to invest in their child's future. Our other adult child and his wife have chosen to invest in advanced language and other enriching educational experiences for their much younger children.

Because our family, like many others, views education as the ultimate escalator not only to a better but also a fuller life, we have chosen to save, gift, and invest in the best educations that our children and grandchildren can access and handle—period, no other questions asked and no promises made. Both of our adult children are well-educated and with no debt for that education. We are truly thankful for the opportunity to have funded their education very early in their lives by regular and systematic gifting.

We have been further blessed by the ability to pursue the same process for each grandchild as they were born, and to commit ourselves to their individual educations all the way through whatever college level they can handle and rise to.

Finally, we have and currently are gifting to several higher educational institutions to provide scholarships for deserving students who are academically qualified but financially needy. The nonmonetary rewards we receive are both a pleasant surprise and a humble privilege.

I share my own story simply to illustrate what seeking financial independence can allow you to do in your life journey, and as simple proof that using money as a positive tool can allow anyone to make their life count for something more than a number.

So, in conclusion, do I recommend the practice of gifting by those who are seeking financial independence? Yes, I do, but not by asking you to adopt my personal preferences or priorities but rather your own, based on what you truly value and how you want to impact the world as you see it.

As an inspiration in the area of gifting, we offer the very old Chinese proverb that, "Giving a man a fish feeds him for a day, but teaching a man to fish feeds him for a lifetime."

Charitable gifting is another way to share financial blessings with others. Under current tax regulations, charitable gifting today can, of course, be in unlimited amounts either during your lifetime or at death, but the current tax advantages are limited and should be verified by your tax advisors. In addition, those who are so inclined can set up various charitable trusts either during their lifetime or at death and thereby can gain some tax advantages while pursuing their charitable intent. We wholeheartedly encourage the use of these various gifting techniques when and where appropriate, and have both professionally and personally used charitable trusts for these purposes.

We believe that the donor should truly have an eleemosynary intent; such charitable activities should not be pursued for purely financial purposes. We would qualify this opinion however by one observation; that is that we are personally firmly opposed to paying federal inheritance tax and accordingly would much prefer to gift away any money that might be going to the federal government at death. This belief is simply based on my contention that taxing money when earned is enough taxation, and we simply choose not to have it taxed again. We do not like the concept that the government gets to decide how much wealth is enough and in effect, how much should be confiscated by the government. Therefore, we prefer to choose for ourselves where our material wealth will ultimately reside and how it will be used.

✓ A financial gift can be an investment in someone else's future for the betterment of that individual or for society in general.

✓ Periodic financial gifts can run the risk of establishing financial dependence.

Epilogue:
Investment Market Reflections and Conclusions

With August fast approaching and another miserably hot summer at its peak, I cannot help but reflect back to that day in August 1967, when as a young man of twenty-seven, I first entered the investment brokerage, financial advisory business. I personally know of only a handful of contemporaries who have been in this business for that length of time, although I am sure there are many more of us around.

It has been a privilege to live my version of the American dream—the same dream that has brought immigrants to our shores for decades. That realization fits very much with my own view of life and eventual retirement (whatever that is and however you might define it). As I have already said, it is far better to be headed toward a destination than away from something. That forward-looking mind-set gives one hope and inspiration, which is after all what life is all about—namely better possibilities.

During the course of my life and business career, it has been my privilege to work with and for hundreds of individuals who, like me, wanted a secure life, a life of opportunity, and a better life for themselves and their families. Together, we have faced the broad sweep of history and ridden the waves of turmoil and time. We were punished by the high inflation period of the late 1970s and early '80s but rode the disinflationary train that followed to a more secure place. We lived through the wasteful years of the Vietnam War and saw our brothers and sisters sacrificed for an ill-defined cause while the nation smoldered both literally and figuratively. We have seen leaders assassinated and our nation attacked by those who hate us. We have survived politicians who pandered to us and played to our baser instincts, but we also have been inspired by others who called upon us to be more just and stronger and responsible, all at the same time.

Our parents, whom Tom Brokaw aptly named "The Greatest Generation," left us a heritage of dedication to self-improvement and societal advancement that still challenges us to rise to their level of dedication to purpose. And yet we still struggle today to see those who will not, cannot, or for whatever reason do not participate in what must be a rededication to American exceptionalism if we are to indeed prosper and grow into our future.

Although my wife and I are fortunate enough to be able to divide our time between homes in Florida and Illinois, I have always deemed it a privilege to have grown up in an ambitious and at times struggling family in America's heartland. The American Midwest is reflective of the nation's historic journey, as we have lived the highs of the industrial growth tidal wave that dominated the US economy through the 1950s and '60s but also witnessed the decline and hollowing out of America's middle and its industrial base that followed. That experience coupled with the incredibly cold and nasty winters makes those who live in this vast space a stronger, more durable, and yes, more adaptable species then many others.

We have not only seen but lived the decline of heavy industry and the rise of global agriculture. The semiconductor was invented right in our midst, and the Internet browser was born at our doorstop, but we have also seen the cost of our collective need to be globally competitive and more relevant.

This collection of lessons was created for several reasons, not the least of which was to give hope and, dare I say, inspiration to younger ones who wonder if there really can be a place for them at the table of prosperity. My belief is that yes, you can still succeed in America like no other place, but you cannot do it with blinders on, and you cannot do it without real grit and determination and the willingness to possibly risk greatly at times. You will likely not reach your goals if you insist on always being part of the crowd and unwilling to stand out even if quietly living by your individual dreams and values regardless of what others might think.

My wish for you is that you achieve your hopefully noble aims by every legitimate means you can employ and be rewarded both materially and spiritually for your life's quest. May it be your good fortune along life's path to know many decent and successful individuals who make up the wonderfully unique American character.

HMF
July 17, 2011

Reference Notes

Past examples of advice to ride the disinflationary train to lower interest rates. These are presented here not to boast about past recommendations but rather to illustrate how what we call long wave opportunities can exist and offer major opportunities to those with conviction and the courage to act on their insight. It is the authors contention that while other long wave investment opportunities have presented themselves during the past several decades, the enormous interest rate peak that existed in the roughly 1979-1983 period was an opportunity for average individual investors to exploit. Accordingly, the following are direct quotes taken from the client newsletters of the author, beginning in October of 1979. For the record, interest rates on US government notes and bonds did not peak until approximately August of 1982.

"Careful, Deliberate Investment Moves Now May Reap Rewards for Conservative Income Investors in the weeks ahead. Many of us view the future through a rear view mirror. In other words, we expect whatever has been happening to continue to happen. I suggest to you that the time for action appears to be at hand. Specifically, I am suggesting that it may be time to invest money with the idea of at least "locking up" for several years the historically high interest rates which exist today. My investment opinion is that the time to move money from short term to longer or intermediate term bond investments is during a maturing period of intense upward pressure on short term interest rates such as appears to exist now and as illustrated in the above inverted yield curve situation."

H. Michael Finkle, Investment Broker
R. Rowland & Co. Incorporated
October 30, 1979

"As regular readers of this letter know, we have been aggressively urging the purchase of long-term bonds to lock in high yields…. With the huge recent market rally, are there any ways left to still lock in double digit interest rates / yes, but not many."

H. Michael Finkle, VP Investment Broker
R. Rowland & Co. Incorporated
October 18, 1982

"Only the borrowers are upset by today's high interest rates....focusing all of these factors into one clear investment picture, I believe calls for investment action now to take advantage of today's attractive yields."

H. Michael Finkle
R. Rowland & Co. Incorporated
June 12, 1984

###

"Is the high interest rate train pulling out ? Obviously no one knows for sure, but at the risk of sounding like a broken record, we believe that a few years from now today's interest rates will look awfully good."

H. Michael Finkle
R. Rowland & Co. Incorporated
July 30, 1984

###

"The federal deficit creates big governmental borrowing at a cost which spells opportunity for investors with cash. I believe that since 1982 there has existed a major opportunity for investors with cash to earn historically unprecedented returns. That opportunity continues today in my opinion.

This reversal of winners and losers in the economic arena has turned the tables in almost all facets of our economic life. Put simply, we have quit rewarding borrowers and started rewarding lenders.

We suggest you should position assets as a lender/investor in any number of US Government securities vehicles.

Sometimes we need to stand back from the daily ups and downs of the marketplace and take the longer view."

H. Michael Finkle
R. Rowland & Co. Incorporated
March 30, 1985

H. Michael Finkle   Vice President|Investments

Blunt Ellis & Loewi   1020 N. Vermilion, Danville, IL 61832 • 217|446-2500 • Nationwide 800|558-1055
Incorporated

Fixed Income Monitor

This report has been compiled as a service to you. Listed below are current offerings
of interest to the conservative income oriented investor.

WALL STREET IS STILL (ALWAYS) A TWO WAY STREET

In recent weeks the financial markets have been worried about an apparently
strong economy reaching the upper limits of its productive capacity. That
translates into fears of inflation creeping up to a higher plateau. The
Wall Street bear consensus calls for inflation to be nearer 5% by year end
than in the 4% to 4 1/2% range of recent years.

Because of the worries over the strength of the economy, interest rates
have been creeping ever so slowly higher. That puts pressure on bond prices
and subsequently the stock market. It is probably not too overstated to
say that bearishness (in this case, fear of higher interest rates) was nearly
unanimous. Everyone with any degree of exposure to the financial world seems
to expect hgiher interest rates. The only debate was over how much higher.

Those of us who have been around awhile, have learned one thing if nothing
else. That is simply that in the long run it is generally easier to make
money going against the crowd rather than running with it. This past Tuesday
and Wednesday, at least, others had come to the same conclusion as prices
in bonds jumped, the stock market rallied broadly, and for a few days, last
week's or last month's worries about inflation, etc. were quieted.

To be certain, this may only be a rally in a bear market, but the lessons
are familiar. When the consensus point of view is lopsided, the fear or
optimism of that consensus is probably already in the market.

Member New York Stock Exchange

H. Michael Finkle   Vice President|Investments

Blunt Ellis & Loewi
Incorporated   1020 N. Vermilion, Danville, IL 61832 • 217|446-2500 • Nationwide 800|558-1055

    For fixed income investors, last week's interest rates had reached a very tempting level. The yield curve has flattened recently as higher long-term rates worked their way down the maturity scale. For example, in May the U. S. Treasury sold a thirty year bond to yield 9.12% and a ten year note to yield 9%. Last week some five year Certificates of Deposit reached 9% yields.

    If inflation stays near 4%, 9% interest earns a 5% "real" rate of return. At 5% inflation, the "real" rate is still 4%. That has been the range for real rates of return in the 1980's – far above the historic ranges.

    If nothing else, the financial market's strong bearishness finally pushed yields high enough last week to pull some cash off the sidelines. The lesson is an old one – Wall Street is still a two way street.

CURRENT YIELDS

Treasury Yield Curve
Yields as of 4:30p.m. Eastern time

10.5% — 5.0% scale, maturities: 3 mos, 6, 1 yr, 2 3 4 5 7 10, 30 maturities

Legend: Yesterday · 1 week ago · 4 weeks ago

Source: Technical Data International

	CD's	Treasuries	Insured Muni's
1 yr.	8.00%	7.43%	--
2 yr.	8.40%	7.97%	--
3 yr.	8.60%	8.19%	--
4 yr.	8.80%	8.36%	--
5 yr.	9.00%	8.49%	5.92%
10 yr.	--	8.93%	6.72%
15 yr.	--	--	7.24%

Please call for current quotes.

Sincerely,

H. Michael Finkle
INVESTMENT BROKER
Vice President/Investments
Blunt Ellis & Loewi

HMF/vi
June 3, 1988

Member New York Stock Exchange

Kemper Securities Group, Inc.
Blunt Ellis & Loewi Division

1020 N. Vermilion
Danville, IL 61832
(217)446-2500
Nationwide: (800)558-1055

H. MICHAEL FINKLE
Senior Vice President/Investments

January 1992

Where do we invest $ now?

Goodbye old year, hello 1992. The past year began with the U.S. going to war in Kuwait and ended with the Russian communist system collapsing. Speaking of collapsing...so did short-term U.S. interest rates.

As the new year begins, short-term interest rates have plunged to 27 year lows. With money market yields at about 4.5%, three-year Treasury rates at 5% and the ten-year Treasury rate under 7%, we are looking at the lowest rates in many people's memory.

As anyone who knows me can tell you, I have been a roaring bull on the bond market since 1982. That's almost a decade now of telling clients to buy longer term bonds and lock in yields to ride the disinflationary economic train. It's been a great ride and it "ain't over yet."

However...no tree grows to the sky, so we have subtly shifted more emphasis toward buying common stocks in recent months. <u>At our annual client seminar in September, we urged every client to put some money into high-quality growth stocks</u>. Our preferred simple way to do that is by purchasing shares of Investment Company of America*.

Just as for years I have urged clients to buy intermediate to longer term bonds and capture the high interest rates of the 1980's, I now urge you to shift <u>some</u> money toward <u>high-quality common stocks</u>. Why buy stocks now? Here is my reasoning:

1. In many recent years, you could capture a very high percentage of the average annual long term return on common stocks (nearly 10% a year**) without taking the same risks. For example, an 8.50% CD or bond, captured 85% of the historic 10% annual return on stocks with a lot less risk! Today, however, you are lucky to find a 7.0% yield which offers only a 70% capture rate compared to stocks using our example.

    So...stocks begin to win the "which should I buy?" argument by default.

2. In 25 years as a broker, I've learned: don't fight the Fed. The Federal Reserve Board's recent huge 1% cut in the discount rate following a string of ¼% cuts underlies their determination to encourage economic growth.

3. I have learned it is usually best to buy stocks in a recession because it's unpopular to do so, business generally "stinks," and pessimism rather than optimism dominates the media. If you think that last point isn't where we are today, just read one newspaper and listen to one TV news broadcast and I assure you, you can get depressed.

So that, dear reader, is my New Year's message. It is an extremely basic and important shift in thinking and strategy for me to make. Without overstating it, I urge you to pick up the phone today and call to discuss your specific situation. Every individual investor and portfolio is a little bit different, so no blanket approach works for everyone. But the message is clear: <u>some shift of emphasis may be needed now so act accordingly, and immediately</u>.

Best wishes for 1992,

[signature]

H. Michael Finkle
Senior Vice President/Investments

*Investment Company of America is a mutual fund offered only by prospectus, available on request.
**Source: Johnson Charts 1991

2832 North Vermilion Suite 1
Danville, IL 61832

toll free 800 390 0025
tel 217 477 0034
fax 217 477 0019

Morgan Stanley

The Finkle-Lewis Team

January 2005

To: Clients of *The Finkle-Lewis Team*

From: The Finkle-Lewis Team of Morgan Stanley

Subject: **Portfolio Strategies & Our Outlook for 2005 and Beyond**

Our long term macro view, formed way back in the early 1980's when Paul Volcker's FED was determined to break the back of U. S. inflation and inflationary psychology, hasn't changed much and has played out pretty well. We have long anticipated the evolvement of a 1950's type environment marked by low interest rates, low inflation and steady trend line growth.

We overlaid this long term picture with the belief that global economic competition and integrations was and is inevitable and irreversible and basically deflationary for the most part.

So here we are, four years into the new millennium, and more or less have arrived at our destination environment with the added wild card of global terrorism thrown in for good measure.

During 2003, all of our advice to clients was based on our conviction that the administration and FED would use massive federal deficits, tax cuts, record low interest rates and a benign dollar policy to successfully re-inflate what was then a rapidly deflating U.S. and developed world economy. That view played out nicely over 2003 and 2004. The policy challenges directly ahead are for a careful pull back of past policies toward a more balanced and slightly less stimulative posture while maintaining adequate U.S. growth near the long term trend line of 3% to 3.5%.

We thus expect short term interest rates to creep higher (50 to 100 basis points) in 2005 and for corporate profit growth to slow to about 8%. That won't necessarily translate into a similar percentage gain in stock prices in 2005 as higher interest rates generally cause PE compression to occur until the FED finishes its work.

We anticipate and accept the consensus view for a lower dollar and for some adjustment of the Chinese currency peg to the dollar. We also believe that longer term, the U.S. must address the trade and budget deficits, plus the domestic savings shortfall and must do whatever it takes to remain globally competitive. In this brave new world, being lean and mean is the key to survival, let alone personal or societal prosperity.

Our micro views include the following.

a) Our now two year old recommendation to **add real estate** (REIT mutual funds) to balanced portfolios has worked out well. We continue to like this asset class for yield and appreciation potential but a great deal of appreciation has already occurred. We recommend limiting exposure to a range of 4% to 8%.

b) Where appropriate (as in large portfolio and most retirement plans), we continue to like **small exposure to commodity mutual funds, funds of funds or strategic allocation funds plus exposure to emerging market bonds and equities** where appropriate. Finally, we have just begun to **add high yield bond exposure**, again. All of these ideas are playing off our 2003-2004 're-inflation trade idea'.

c) We continue to emphasize **dividend income from stocks** and a strong preference for a **value style stock selection** and management system attempting to control capital risks through below index volatility (beta) and increased investment cash flow.

d) While the FED normalizes short term interest rates and currency realignment is likely, large domestic stocks are likely to generate returns below their long term average levels of 10-11%, with maybe 7% a more realistic number. **Global equities on the other hand look cheaper and could well outperform domestic stocks**. We also think it highly unlikely for high grade bonds to repeat their 2004 gains in the face of the market forces we expect.

These views are precisely why we are working harder than ever to increase cash flow, dampen volatility in your major allocation categories and add asset diversity by trying to tactically add the asset classes referenced above seeking lower correlations to the normal stock/bond mix.

This environment we now live in isn't unexpected, but it is very different from the past and requires a more sophisticated approach to profit from. Thus we have increased our efforts to more broadly diversify portfolios to reflect our world view as partially outlined herein. Part of this effort has resulted in our decision to expand The Finkle-Lewis Team professional staff. We have added two important people to our professional staff this year and are now more focused than ever before on servicing and meeting your investment needs!

We look forward to speaking with you about your individual investment needs in the weeks ahead. You have helped us to grow our business significantly and we are making substantial investments in both people and systems to earn even more of your business. Rest assured that we are focused, committed and fully engaged in making The Finkle-Lewis Team the best investment services team we possibly can.

Sincerely,

H. Michael Finkle
Senior Vice President, Wealth Advisor
Estate Planning Consultant
Retirement Planning Specialist

Barbara L. Lewis
Associate Vice President, Financial Advisor
Estate Planning Consultant
Retirement Planning Specialist

RATE OF CAPITAL GROWTH AT
COMPOUND INTEREST

(Compounding Semi-Annually)
$100 a Month Savings

Rate %	10 Years	15 Years	20 Years	25 Years	30 Years
2	$13,211	$20,871	$29,332	$38,678	$49,002
2½	13,538	21,677	30,894	41,329	53,145
3	13,874	22,523	32,561	44,210	57,729
3½	14,221	23,410	34,340	47,341	62,805
4	14,578	24,341	36,241	50,747	68,431
4½	14,947	25,317	38,272	54,455	74,670
5	15,327	26,342	40,442	58,490	81,595
5½	15,718	27,417	42,761	62,887	89,285
6	16,122	28,545	45,241	67,678	97,832
6½	16,538	29,730	47,893	72,902	107,336
7	16,968	30,974	50,730	78,599	117,910
7½	17,410	32,279	53,766	84,815	129,682
8	17,867	33,651	57,016	91,600	142,795
8½	18,338	35,092	60,494	99,009	157,407
9	18,823	36,604	64,218	107,102	173,699
9½	19,324	38,194	68,207	115,944	191,872
10	19,840	39,863	72,480	125,609	212,150
10½	20,372	41,618	77,058	136,175	234,788
11	20,921	43,461	81,964	147,730	260,070
11½	21,487	45,398	87,221	160,371	288,314
12	22,072	47,435	92,857	174,202	319,877

TAX RATES

Taxable income is income after all deductions, including either itemized deductions or the standard deduction, and exemptions.

FEDERAL INDIVIDUAL INCOME TAX RATES

Married Taxpayer Joint / Surviving Spouse

Taxable Income	Pay	Percentage on Excess	Of Amount Above
Less than $17,000	N/A	10%	$0
17,000 – 69,000	$1,700.00	15	17,000
69,000 – 139,350	9,500.00	25	69,000
139,350 – 212,300	27,087.50	28	139,350
212,300 – 379,150	47,513.50	33	212,300
More than 379,150	102,574.00	35	379,150

Single Taxpayer

Taxable Income	Pay	Percentage on Excess	Of Amount Above
Less than $8,500	N/A	10%	$0
8,500 – 34,500	$850.00	15	8,500
34,500 – 83,600	4,750.00	25	34,500
83,600 – 174,400	17,025.00	28	83,600
174,400 – 379,150	42,449.00	33	174,400
More than 379,150	110,016.50	35	379,150

Head of Household

Taxable Income	Pay	Percentage on Excess	Of Amount Above
Less than $12,150	N/A	10%	$0
12,150 – 46,250	$1,215.00	15	12,150
46,250 – 119,400	6,330.00	25	46,250
119,400 – 193,350	24,617.50	28	119,400
193,350 – 379,150	45,323.50	33	193,350
More than 379,150	106,637.50	35	379,150

Personal Exemption – $3,700

The phase out for personal exemptions and itemized deductions has been eliminated through 2012.

Standard Deduction – Single $5,800;
Head of Household $8,500; Joint $11,600

*Extra Deduction if blind or over 65 – Single or head of household $1,450, All Other Statuses $1,150

III. KEY TAX RULES

DIVIDEND AND CAPITAL GAINS RATES

Individual Dividend Rates

	Maximum Rate	Rate for Qualified Dividends*
Taxpayers Above the 15% Bracket	35%	15%
Taxpayers in the 15% Bracket and Below	15%	0%

*"Qualified dividends" generally refers to dividends received during 2011 from domestic corporations. The investor must own the stock for more than 60 days during the 120-day period beginning 60 days before the ex-dividend date. These periods are doubled for preferred securities.

Appendix
and Disclosures by the Author

Views expressed in this publication are the current opinion of the author and are subject to change without notice. Information contained in this book was received from sources believed to be reliable, but accuracy is not guaranteed.

Investors should consider the investment objectives, risks, and charges and expenses of exchange-traded products and mutual funds carefully before investing. A prospectus which contains this and other information about these funds can be obtained by contacting your financial advisor. Please read the prospectus carefully before investing.

Past performance is not indicative of future results. Investing always involves risk, and you may incur a profit or loss. No investment strategy can guarantee success.

The S&P 500 is an unmanaged index of 500 widely held stocks. It is not possible to invest directly in an index.

Standard deviation is a risk statistic used to measure the amount of volatility of the return observations around the portfolio's average return.

There is an inverse relationship between interest rate movements and fixed income prices. Generally, when interest rates rise, fixed income prices fall; when interest rates fall, fixed income prices generally rise.

High-yield bonds are not suitable for all investors. The risk of default may increase due to changes in the issuer's credit quality. Price changes may occur due to changes in interest rates and the liquidity of the bond. When appropriate, these bonds should only comprise a modest portion of your portfolio.

Foreign investments often involve special risks not present in US investments that can increase the chances of loss. Among these potential risks are politically and economically unstable environments; greater price volatility; comparatively weak supervision and regulation of securities exchanges, brokers, and issuers; higher brokerage costs; fluctuations in foreign currency exchange rates and related conversion costs; adverse tax consequences; and settlement delays. These risks are greater in emerging markets.

Commodity trading is generally considered speculative because of the significant potential for investment loss. Markets for commodities are likely to be volatile and there may be sharp price fluctuations even during periods when prices overall are rising. The value of commodity-linked derivative investments may be affected by changes in overall market movements; commodity index volatility; changes in interest rates or sectors affecting a particular industry or commodity (such as drought, floods, weather, embargoes, tariffs); and international economic, political, and regulatory developments.

REITs are financial vehicles that pool investors' capital to purchase or finance real estate. REITs may concentrate their investments in specific geographic areas or in specific property types, i.e., hotels, shopping malls, residential complexes, and office buildings. The value of the REITs and the ability of the REITs to distribute income may be adversely affected by several factors including rising interest rates; changes in the national, state, and local economic climate and real-estate conditions; perceptions of prospective tenants of the safety, convenience, and attractiveness of the properties; the ability of the owner to provide adequate management, maintenance, and insurance; the cost of complying with the Americans with Disabilities Act;

increased competition from new properties; the impact of present or future environmental legislation and compliance with environmental laws; changes in real-estate taxes and other operating expenses; adverse changes in governmental rule and fiscal policies; adverse changes in zoning laws; and other factors beyond the control of the issuers of the REITs.

Diversification and strategic/tactical asset allocation do not ensure a profit or protect against a loss. Investments are subject to market risk, including possible loss of principal.

Small and medium-size companies have limited product lines or markets. They may be less financially secure than larger, more established companies and may depend on a more limited management group. Consequently, investments in the securities of these companies may experience greater price volatility.

Changes in tax laws may occur at any time and could have a substantial impact upon each person's situation. Readers should always consult with a qualified tax advisor prior to making any investment decision.

Dividends are not guaranteed and will fluctuate.

Master Limited Partnership (MLP) distributions are not guaranteed. The actual amount of cash distributions may fluctuate and will depend on the future operating performance. Increasing interest rates could have an adverse effect on MLP unit prices as alternative yields become more attractive. Past performance is not indicative of future results.

Alternative investments involve specific risks that may be greater than those associated with traditional investments and may be offered only to clients who meet specific suitability requirements, including minimum net worth tests. You should consider the special risks with alternative investments including limited liquidity, tax considerations, incentive fee structures, potentially speculative investment strategies, and different regulatory and reporting requirements. You should only invest in hedge funds, managed futures, or other similar strategies if you do not require a liquid investment and can bear the risk of substantial losses. There can be no assurance that any investment will meet its performance objectives or that substantial losses will be avoided.

Biotechnology companies are affected by patent considerations, intense competition, rapid technology change and obsolescence, and regulatory requirements.

H. Michael Finkle
June 29, 2011